Smile At Your Challenges

It takes more than just going gluten-free, drinking green juice, and practicing yoga to solve your problems

Danielle Pashko

ISBN: 1494949040
ISBN 13: 9781494949044

For becoming the woman I am today,
I dedicate this book to the memory of my mother, Louise,
and to her dearest friend, Beverly,
who has loved and encouraged me
like her own daughter.

I would like to also acknowledge
the advice, love and support of the following people:

Dr. Landon Agoado and his lovely wife Shari; his brother Dr. Andrew Agoado, all whom I adore as my own siblings; Penny Aryeh the owner of APM models that I first worked for at 16 and has become like a big sister and best friend; MJ Pedone of Indra PR - my angel who convinced me to write this book; Andre' Weinfeld, a great friend and marketing genius who always believed in my talent; and my very patient editor Christina Hamlett who now knows me better than anyone after reading my life story 1000 times.

The spiritual teachers and mentors I have so much gratitude for that may not even realize what influence they have had on my life path: Lewis Harrison, Eddie Stern, Evan Perry, Joshua Rosenthal, Rabbi Mark Wildes, Rebbetzin Esther Jungreis, Chani Pearlman, Eitan Yardeni, and Dr. Oz Garcia.

Table of Contents

Foreword

Happiness is an inside job.

Yes, you read that correctly. You can have all the trappings of success – the house, the car, the closet full of designer labels, membership in all of the best clubs, and the admiration of friends and colleagues – but none of it will ignite your passion, warm your heart or feed your soul if you're expecting happiness to be brought to you by someone else.

It goes without saying that each and every one of us is a product of our past upbringing and our current environment, a potent combination that all too often causes us to be shaped and defined by the expectations of others. It's a script that takes many forms – "You'll never be as beautiful as your older sister," "Your father was a loser and so are you," "When I was your age, I was _____," "You owe it to this family to follow in my footsteps." We may have long since left childhood behind but those critical voices that create fear, instill guilt, and erode self-confidence have a way of tightly attaching themselves for the journey throughout adulthood.

Whether it's a spouse, coworker or boss who triggers our defense mechanisms through their fault-finding, labeling or even neglect, the immediate and most common reaction is to assume that if we can just "fix" ourselves enough, we will no longer be flawed in the eyes of others.

And so we diet. We exercise. We meditate. We juice. We cleanse. We visualize. We pray. We seek therapy. We take medications. We buy new wardrobes. We change our hair color. We marry. We divorce. We change jobs. We relocate.

Yet when we take a step back to assess the results of all these major makeover campaigns, we're still left wondering, "So where's the happy that was supposed to happen? Why isn't it here yet?"

The truth is that it's been inside of you from the get-go and just waiting for you to acknowledge its right to be heard, trusted and manifested. That's what makes the book you're holding in your hands at this moment such an invaluable gem. It's not only delivered through the eyes, wisdom and savvy business acumen of someone whose own journey was far from smooth but also through the awareness that every lesson, every challenge and even every setback is something worth smiling about. Why? Because you're one step closer to figuring out why you're really here. And once you do, don't be surprised to discover that happiness has taken up permanent residence.

Replete with anecdotes and observations about the human condition, this is a book that invites thoughtful consideration of our relationships with others, our relationship with a higher power and, most importantly, the ongoing relationship we nurture – or should be nurturing - with our own selves.

If your inner voice up until now has been lamenting, "Why me?" Danielle's no-nonsense approach to dealing with life's curveballs will change your mind set to, "Why not?" At the end of the day, who better than you knows what you want, why you want it, and what sacrifices and leaps of faith you're prepared to take in order to get it.

Oz Garcia, Ph.D.
Author, Nutritionist, Wellness Expert

one

You Don't Have to Wear Your Pain

"A girl should be two things," wrote Coco Chanel, "classy and fabulous."

Unfortunately, I think too many people attach these qualities to a sizable bank account - or social pedigree - rather than to the idea of having a proud and gracious demeanor. At a young age I realized that money and class were not the same thing, perhaps one of the greatest lessons I ever learned from the classiest woman I ever knew: my mother.

She grew up in The Rockaway projects of New York, the daughter of a mentally ill mother and an unknown father. She couldn't wait to turn 18 and get married just so she could put this troubling situation behind her. Rather than pursue a career, she had me and became a parent.

Her lack of job skills soon came back to bite her when she and my father divorced and she was forced to become a waitress, the only thing that paid enough to support both of us. My mother was a woman who busted her ass working day and night and yet half the time couldn't afford a babysitter. At only seven or eight years old, I was what you'd call a *latchkey kid* who typically came home to an empty house, made a sandwich and watched Oprah or Phil Donahue.

Despite the lack of adult supervision during these formative years, I was mature for my age and uncharacteristically responsible. I also thought this sort of life was normal and, in some ways, liked my routine and independence.

Everything changed a few years later when my mother began developing health problems. The diagnosis was breast cancer, and it quickly became clear that she couldn't maintain the demanding physical workload of waitressing. Gary, the man who would become my stepfather, came into the picture during the early stages of her disease. I wish I could say he was kind and took care of her but this wasn't the case. Yes, he brought money to the table but he was extremely abusive. Anyone who might have thought it was wonderful for him to marry a woman with cancer didn't know that it was just part of his dark agenda to profit from her insurance money.

My mother had always been beautiful. When she became sick, I couldn't comprehend how "young" early 30's was, much less grasp how much tragedy she had endured and how many hits she had taken during her short life. As she got worse, her looks began to decline. The medications made her face bloated and distorted, the chemotherapy caused her to lose her hair, and she no longer had breasts from her double mastectomy. I remember having to push her up the stairs every night to her second floor bedroom because she had trouble moving around.

Yet unbelievably – and despite everything she was experiencing - she had great style and grace that never belied the extreme pain of her condition. She'd never leave the house, for instance, without being impeccably dressed (on a TJ Maxx budget.) She always wore nail polish and a full face of makeup with red lipstick. Her wig was so real looking that it fooled everyone. I still laugh to this day about how she always had to smell good and loved piling on the perfume, even at the expense of reeking like a French whore!

She died in hospice on Mother's Day – May 10, 1992. She was wearing a wig, makeup, and had a bottle of mouthwash under her bed.

* * *

I took a lead from my mother's example and always made sure to be well put together in public. To clarify, that never meant a full face of makeup with blown-out hair. Typically, though, you won't see me walk out of the house without a little mascara, blush, and my hair in a bun or soft pony tail if it's not cooperating with the weather. Whether you're going to your neighborhood Starbucks, the grocery store, or taking a flight to see your grandmother in Florida, you never know who you might run into. It's always those times when you cross paths with someone you least expected – a person you do business with, a handsome single guy, or an ex-boyfriend – that you just want to sink through the pavement for letting them see you unhappy or like crap.

* * *

Before my thyroid cancer was diagnosed in 2009, I couldn't handle working a full-time office job because of my constant sickness and exhaustion. I felt so worn out. I even thought at one point that I was actually dying. Ironically, that never stopped me from getting up every day, pulling myself together from head to toe, and smiling. Based on the way I presented myself, everyone thought that I was just fine or even actually great. It was never my intention to fool everyone to such a degree but apparently because my appearance wasn't suffering, I was even approached by a photographer to get back into the modeling industry.

I thought, "Maybe I should pursue this modeling opportunity so I can still have an income and be able to quit my 9-5 nutritional sales position. I can always rest in between castings, and it's not like I'm going to be booked all the time."

The days that I was booked for modeling jobs - even with as bad as I felt, it was usually offset by the fabulous hair dressers and makeup artists that would glam me out. They were really flamboyant and would tell me hysterical stories about all their boyfriend dramas - exactly the kind of mindless conversation and humor I needed to take me out of my current pain. When I looked in the mirror and saw my transformation, I'd instantly feel better. It's crazy how a woman can feel like shit, but with a little makeover she can suddenly feel like a million bucks!

* * *

On March 18 2010, I was scheduled for my thyroid surgery at Memorial Sloan-Kettering Cancer Center. I was terrified and have always hated hospitals because of spending so much time in them with my mother. I began freaking out in the elevators at the sight of patients in wheel-chairs or those who were hairless from their chemo treatments.

Despite the fact I have 5,000 Facebook friends and a lively social life, I didn't really tell anyone I knew about what was happening to me because I didn't want them to feel sorry for me. That said, most my time in the hospital room was spent alone.

I was completely drugged up following the surgery. The nurse told me I couldn't use my phone in the recovery room. I have no idea what I was thinking or what the urgency was, but I hid my Blackberry under my blanket and started sending out very strange emails and text messages to work clients and friends, not to tell them that I was in the hospital but just to make small talk. I think I was subconsciously lonely and wanted connection. When I later re-read what I sent, it made me laugh and I apologized for the "crazy talk" and misspellings. It was definitely the morphine speaking...

After the nurses wheeled me back to my room, I didn't want to stay in bed. Being high as a kite and wobbling about, I took my makeup case into the bathroom and started brushing my hair and putting on a little bronzer, mascara, and lip gloss. It sounds dumb - maybe even superficial - but I didn't want to look in the mirror and see a sick girl. Seeing a healthy-looking reflection - even if it was fake, thanks to the makeup - made me feel like I was going to get better again soon.

* * *

Between being put on medication and having radiation treatments, it took about a year for my body to start adjusting back to a normal state. I still had a lot of really bad days but definitely pushed myself. I even forced myself to go out on dates and keep commitments with friends.

To this day, many people who have known me over the years through work, my community, or very close circles didn't know what I went through. It drives me crazy to see people walk around with what my mother would call a "sourpuss" face. They don't realize that eventually their external expressions will take over who they are; by default, everything about them becomes miserable, possibly even creating illness.

Even when we feel like our world is crumbling, we need to work on looking our best and smiling. People are attracted to other positive people. Everyone has challenges but if we wear our problems for the world to see, we're holding ourselves back from overcoming them.

two

Beauty is a Blessing and a Curse

"I wish you the luck of the ugly girls," a friend of mine once said to me. It was actually a very profound statement. I think it's generally assumed that if you're pretty, life is easy and you can get away with a lot more. There are definite perks but there's often an accompanying boatload of problems that most people never consider.

Once the advent of Facebook made it possible for me to start looking up friends I had lost track of, I was amazed by how many of those who were average-looking are not only happy, confident, and fulfilled in their marriages but already on their second or third kid. On the flip side, the girlfriends who fit every possible definition of "hot" are still single.

To be honest, I've never had a problem attracting the opposite sex. Men would invite me to business meetings, social events, and even on their travels since I always made an appropriate date. Translated: I was playing the arm-candy role of "trophy." It was also clear to me that many of these men would do and say anything to get me in bed. Absent any genuine connection, there was also never any chance for my inner beauty to be revealed. It wasn't that I didn't like the nice guys, the ones who might have truly cared about my interests and opinions. In fact I genuinely prayed for one of those good guys to come into my path. Unfortunately those weren't the ones who approached me. From speaking with other men, there is something to being intimated by attractive women. Guys who were confident and cocky usually were the only ones with the balls to ask me out.

In retrospect, it's as if the men I dated made a distinction between two types of women: the hot chick you had fun with (and who represented novelty), and the girl next door that you could take home to meet mom (and eventually marry). In the 1960's, *Gilligan's Island* even contributed a catchphrase for this syndrome: "Ginger or Mary Ann?"

Although I was definitely not your typical girl next door, my personality traits and core values – especially sensitivity, honesty and empathy - were more fitting that character than the high maintenance woman I was inaccurately perceived to be.

* * *

Men aren't the only ones who rush to false judgments based on a person's physical appearance. Females are just as guilty of this offense, something which I first discovered during childhood.

For starters, I had a mole on my face. In the 90's Cindy Crawford was the top model at the time so I was fine with it- but the girls at my elementary school would tell me it looked like a cockroach. I was also the butt of many jokes about my height – 5 feet 10 inches at 13 years old. While I could laugh it off as ridiculous when they resorted to calling me names like "Big Bird" or "Jolly Green Giant," being singled out for teasing because of a physical attribute over which I had no control, carried connotations that I was woefully flunking some arbitrary standard of "normal."

As a teenager, I bounced around to four different high schools. Accordingly, whenever I switched to a different setting, I was always the "new girl." New girls are typically viewed with a mix of curiosity and suspicion. What's her deal? Where did she come from? Why is she here? She thinks she's hot shit because she's pretty. It's the latter assumption that sealed my fate in the classroom… and beyond. Unless you're accepted and absorbed into the controlling clique on campus, there's no one to protect you, to speak up for you, to keep you company.

* * *

As a sophomore, I started attending Forest Hills High in Queens to live with an aunt and uncle. I had just come from Florida where the girls were a little sexier, fit, and a lot better groomed than the new crowd I was walking into. Because of my height I could easily pass for 21. I remember my first day of school. I wanted to look stylish so I decided to wear white fitted jeans and high boots. Maybe the white was a faux pas after Labor Day. What did I know? I had a pretty good tan, my hair blown out straight and a French manicure. My favorite perfume was called "Design" and I sprayed on just a little before walking out the door. My fashion sense was very L.A. or Miami and I'd venture to say even a little cheesy. Because I came from a beach and body conscious culture, I was used to being shaved in personal places and wearing thong underwear with all my clothes was the norm. The girls in gym class at Forest Hills High were the complete opposite. Note to self: Queens girls are not beach girls! The closest city beaches were with dirty water and unidentified objects floating in them such as diapers or needles. The first time we got undressed in the locker room, my ass was hanging out and the other girls were wearing what I considered "grandma underwear" with a bush coming out the sides. You can imagine how I became the talk of the school!

It's ironic how I used to think the girls from my other high schools were too focused on fashion or their appearance and yet that's exactly what I was being judged for. I had secretly copied their sense of style in an effort to fit in with them but the look clearly wasn't flying. The one thing going for me was that I was a decent athlete. My only hope was to try out for the basketball team to have protection against getting my ass kicked. I also had to downplay the clothes I wore as a way to deflect negative attention. With some help from Betty - the only girl who took me under her wing - I changed from being what I thought was cute and trendy to dressing like a "home girl" out of a Salt N Pepa video. The safer look for me became baggy jeans and shirts with bamboo earrings. Overnight I started looking like a New Yorker or, rather, a Queens girl which is very different from Manhattan. The new makeover didn't last long, though. I felt ridiculous, a little immature and unsophisticated. Instead I started copying the style of the other girls in Soho and The Village so I'd look like a cool city girl and get rid of the big sign on my head that said "out of towner." I really respect New York girls for looking so fabulous and put together without showing skin or having their boobs hanging out.

When I moved out of my aunt and uncles apartment at 16, and began paying my own rent while attending high school, it was hard for people to comprehend how I could support myself beyond being a model, stripper or finding a rich boyfriend. Although I was a great student, articulate, and had a good head on my shoulders, from where they stood, it appeared that my looks would always be my ticket to survival.

* * *

One thing I often dealt with was that when you're pretty, less people have sympathy for you even if your life is very difficult. Look at someone like Elizabeth Taylor. She always had a crisis going on – serious health problems, divorces, etc. – but the world wasn't crying for her because she was also glamorous and beautiful. No matter what pain she was enduring, people were still envious of her looks.

My circumstance was that I was a teenager struggling without parents and without any money but everyone still saw my life as charmed. Even when I became very sick in my late 20's, the doctors didn't believe my case. They thought that because I "looked good" my illness was all in my head. I was sent to several psychiatrists and was labeled as a crazy girl who made up her symptoms. I was accused of being anorexic for reasons of vanity when, in fact, I was not starving myself; I had cancer.

Even with all of the chaos throughout my life, many who don't know me are quick to judge that I'm no more than just a pretty face. Plenty of my accomplishments have taken a backseat to others' misperceptions.

Don't always think that the pretty girl has won the lottery. When there's luck in one area, many times there is lack in another. When you look in the mirror, try not to only focus on your physical reflection - but recognize all the inner qualities that make you beautiful.

three

Just be Yourself

During elementary school was when it first became obvious I was different. I was the only Jewish kid in a poor minority neighborhood in a place called North Lauderdale Florida. The only other white children I encountered were rednecks who were so brainwashed that they would ask me if I had horns and say crazy things like I was going to Hell if I didn't accept Jesus. Not only did I feel like an alien, but I never got to run around and do normal things like playing because I had to be the grown-up looking after my sick mother. Because of my adult responsibilities I was socially awkward and had no clue how to relate to other kids, how to be light and carefree, or how to be youthful.

Whatever expectations I might have had about fitting in once I reached high school in New York clearly never manifested. While everyone else was super focused on their SAT scores or dates to the prom, my priority was to make money to be able to support myself. I was already living with a roommate but wanted my own place. I began a work study program and got to leave school early every day. I was one of those students who could pull in good grades even if I didn't study or skipped class (which I often did because of my hectic work schedule). I worked as a hostess/bartender at night despite being underage. After school I'd run around on casting calls hoping to book modeling jobs to bring in extra money.

Within a few months I had saved up enough to move to Manhattan and rent a small studio on the Upper Westside. I had a crazy deal of only $500 a month in what was called a doorman building. (It was actually a hotel efficiency.) It was decorated with old chandeliers, dim, depressing lighting, and felt totally creepy and haunted. The building number was unbelievably 666 West End Avenue! Even though I once contemplated calling in an exorcist after some bazaar paranormal activity, I kick myself to this day for giving up that cheapo rent. Every morning I made the reverse commute to school in Queens at 5:30 a.m. It was a seedy ride on the subway from 96th and Broadway. Even as tired as I was from bartending some nights and not even having time to sleep, I struggled to stay awake on the #1 train out of fear of getting mugged or possibly worse.

* * *

As a senior in high school I was pulled into fast circles - and it wasn't with the kids from my school. I was invited out by club promoters every night of the week. This was the entertainment that for me and other young models or tall, pretty girls that would cost less than the price of a movie ticket. I would never wait in line behind a velvet rope or pay admission. Some of the other perks were free meals, unlimited alcohol, and cocaine if I wanted it. For the record, I never put anything in my nose because I was afraid of my mortality after seeing what happened to my mom. I also didn't sleep around with a strong fear of diseases for the same reasons.

Although I ran with the party crowd, it came across that I was a good girl who wouldn't succumb to peer pressure. People felt shame in doing really dark things in my presence. I'd be at a night club, for instance, and I knew everyone was doing lines of coke but they tried to keep it hidden from me. While being the youngest in the group, I was always respected and had this very parental kind of energy. Often random acquaintances 10 years my senior would cut out their bullshit air of coolness and then, for no reason, they would start telling me their life story, inadequacies or something very deep and personal. Rather than go along with the group and their actions, I connected better on a one-on-one basis, but it was usually playing the role of therapist. For example people opened up to me about being secretly bi-sexual, sexual abuse from relatives, how they got into drugs, children they had but never parented, I heard it all. Additionally, these people would also share their unmet aspirations of doing more with their life which made me feel kind of sorry for them. Although I appreciated being recognized for my insight, I felt like I was with a group of vampires that were sucking my energy and pure spirit. Their actions were just too reckless for my comfort.

As I got to know more people from living in Manhattan, I would get invitations to The Hamptons. This was where most of the people who had money would go to escape the summer heat of the city. The houses cost a fortune and many of them were rented or purchased from young finance guys or trust fund kids. There were also "share houses" with more down-to-earth people, but I didn't want to shack up in a house with 20 other people who wanted the Hamptons experience without actually being able to afford it. My friends would go out and blow money like nothing. Just going to the store to buy a few things for a barbeque would easily be a few hundred dollars; dinners with a few friends could be in the thousands.

I was never able to contribute to anything other than offer pleasant conversation and good company. I felt seriously poor. I didn't have the money like the other girls who wore all the designer clothes. While they were sporting the hot brands at the time - Prada bags, Gucci shoes, and Dolce and Gabbana dresses and swimsuits - I didn't own one single thing with a designer label and it was definitely obvious. I was struggling just to pay for the cost of the Hampton Jitney - my transportation back and forth. After the bus fare, I was usually left with under $50 in my pocket to cover me for the entire weekend! It became clear I wasn't of the same social pedigree, but believed I had all the potential to become a success and have a nice bank account someday. Although I knew that when that day came, material possessions and social status wouldn't hold so much importance.

* * *

After spending my first summer in The Hamptons I needed a new circle of friends and dropped out of the Chi-Chi world for a bit. To add balance to my life, I started practicing yoga and changed my environment. It was like a breath of fresh air. Not just because it was healthy, but because it wasn't superficial. Yoga is meant to be the opposite of Ego - exactly what I had been surrounded by in every direction. Class was the one place I could go without the need to pretend or impress anyone, (I could roll out of bed in my pajamas to practice if I felt like it) and no one would say a thing. At that time, yoga also hadn't gained the popularity like it has today. Back then, it was attracting a certain kind of person that was drawn to improving themselves spiritually rather than being a fad. There wasn't any emphasis on who you knew, what you did for a living, or what you were wearing - very different from the current LuLu Lemon culture of matching shorts and top, fancy yoga bag, and a tote for your Chihuahua. Still, if this gets the mainstream to be excited about lifting their consciousness then I'm all for it. Hopefully the lessons of spirituality that are being taught in class are still recognized as more important than just "looking cool" and being trendy.

It's easy to follow the crowd, but I'd rather beat to my own drum. It took a long time to become comfortable in my own skin and not try to fit where I don't belong. There's a disease that many people we all know are plagued with called "FOMO – Fear Of Missing Out." You know what? If you're happy with yourself, you're not missing anything!

four

Picture of Health

In order to be truly healthy, don't discount that our spiritual and emotional well-being is even more important than diet and exercise. There are a million doctors, nutritionists, yoga instructors and health coaches that sometimes miss this crucial reality.

In the early stages of my wellness career I was one of those rah rah people that only ate things which were green or fell from a tree, and often did two workouts in one day. In the mornings I'd practice yoga and if I had time in the evening I'd likely do a run or lift some weights at the gym. I've always liked control and believed that if I kept up this routine forever I'd live to see 100!

Because my mother passed so early, I thought maybe somehow her lack of exercise and poor eating habits led to her cancer. The only time I saw her do something physical was to vacuum the apartment while dancing around to Donna Summer. Back in the 80's and 90's, of course, most women weren't working out at gyms like they do today. My mom never ate salads or was health conscious in the least bit. Her idea of good nutrition was eating a Weight Watchers meal or drinking a Slim Fast.

I made a decision after she died that I would outsmart her. In addition to living on mostly fruit, vegetables, tofu and lentils, I had made my own strict rules of no sugar, no meat, no wheat, no dairy, and no alcohol. This was years before the holistic lifestyle became super trendy.

I maintained this rigid existence throughout all of my 20's. My social life would also revolve around my workout schedule. That meant

I never wanted to stay out late or be awakened for sex in the middle of the night because I may, God forbid, feel tired in the morning and have a shitty yoga practice. Lights went out at 9:30 p.m. and I was up and out the door around 5 a.m., even when it was still dark out and freezing.

Looking back, if I were a man I wouldn't have dated someone like me. I lived with such discipline in all areas in my life that friends would joke around and tell me I could be a commander in the military. Fun for me was secondary; it was all about excelling and achieving physical strength and perfection.

As my career advanced, I'd deal with all kinds of clients but sometimes with frustration. If my yoga students lacked stamina, I felt like they were being lazy. If I had a nutrition client that was very overweight, I thought I would just get them off processed food, white bread, and sugar - problem solved. What I discovered, however, is that it wasn't so clear-cut. Being in shape looked so easy for me that they probably felt like I couldn't possibly relate to their circumstances or knew what it felt like to be in their body for a second.

They were right. Until my own health problems crept up and eventually led to a thyroid cancer diagnosis, I actually had no idea what it was like to not be a picture of health.

* * *

In 2008 I had a crazy work and social schedule. I was working full-time with a well known alternative medical doctor. I was also exploring my Judaism and devoted my evenings to doing a one-year program with a rabbi at my synagogue. While that was happening, I put unnecessary pressure on myself to get remarried after my recent divorce.

So this is how my days went down:

5 a.m. –   Wake up and travel downtown to practice yoga, come back uptown to my apartment to shower.

9 a.m. –   Travel back downtown to start work.

6 p.m. –   Leave work, go home, scarf down a salad and rush to The Upper West Side.

7-9:15 p.m. – Attend religious classes. Freshen up and change in the synagogue bathroom.

9:30 p.m. – Get picked up for a date that would usually last until 11 pm.

11:30 p.m. – Get home, wash up, go to bed.

Repeat all of the above the very next day.

I didn't miss a beat and this went on for a long time. I was going to bed much later than before because I was now single and dating was a priority and second job. If I just cut back on my workouts, I would have felt better than waking up before dawn.

I thought I was doing an okay job of managing my life until my boss, the doctor, said to me, "You are walking a slippery slope." He was observing that I seemed frazzled, anxious, and overtired. In addition, I was internally panicked because my male suitors were just not working out. I must have gone on 30 dates that year and didn't feel excited by anyone. The combination of my day-to-day schedule, demanding workouts with too little sleep to recover, and the fear of never connecting with someone set me off and put my adrenals into total burnout.

Even with my so called perfect diet and yoga routine, my health was on the decline. One of the treatments our offices gave to patients was IV drips that were infused with vitamins. I started feeling so bad physically that I asked the nurses to administer it to me. I would sit at my desk and get hooked up to an IV bag with B vitamins for energy, vitamin C for my immune system to deal with stress, and nutrients like magnesium and inositol to help with the anxiety. It provided short term relief - enough to get me through the work day. But then new problems started showing up.

* * *

After my classes and dates in the evening, I was no longer able to fall asleep. I was dead tired and ready to sleep, but while lying in the dark bedroom I was unable to shut down. It felt like torture because I would get so close to passing out and suddenly for no reason my body would go into fight or flight mode as if my house was on fire and hit me with a surge of adrenalin. I would watch the clock and as it got into 2 a.m. and 3 a.m., I knew I had to be up soon. The fear and sometimes crying from exhaustion would perpetuate the insomnia. By the time I finally fell asleep, the alarm would wake me up in two hours. With such little rest, I was no longer capable of doing yoga or any form of workout at all for that matter.

Meanwhile, part of my job responsibility was health writing. I would get called to do a piece for a magazine on, for instance, sleep hygiene. This was ironic, wasn't it? I knew everything you were *supposed* to do - no caffeine, no television or computer in bed, only use the bedroom for sex or sleeping, don't nap during the day, keep the air temperature cold, and keep room as dark as possible. As I'm writing quickly to make the editor's deadline, I'm thinking "check, check, check, check, check" on all of my tips but none of them are working for me.

At first I was committed to taking care of my sleep problem the holistic way. I tried melatonin, GABA, 5-HTP, tryptophan, and seeing an acupuncturist twice a week. I even went to see a healer that did crystal therapy and hypnosis but all of that stuff did absolutely nothing except run up bills I could barely afford.

I needed the hammer effect and couldn't believe that me – "Miss Natural Health" - was about to resort to using prescription drugs. It was a tough decision but it was either that or put a gun to my head from sleep deprivation. I was alternating between Ambien and Lunesta while adding a bunch of tranquilizers and benzos to my repertoire. The doses I became addicted to should have knocked out a 500 pound man and sometimes did nothing to sedate my fragile 110 pound 5'10" frame. In addition to not sleeping, I got so skinny that a stiff wind could have blown me over.

When I finally got to the bottom of why this was all happening and how it related to my cancer diagnosis, I knew that my stress and hectic lifestyle played a big role in my symptoms. Now when I deal with clients, it's so clear that emotional state, sleep, stress, lifestyle, and in depth diagnostic testing to uncover underlined hidden health issues, all need to be taken into consideration before just advising someone to become a vegan, go macrobiotic, drink green juice, or take up yoga.

After three years of recovery, I feel terrific but have also completely switched my life around. I still exercise daily but not on a schedule. I no longer have a 5 a.m. routine nor will I ever again! I do yoga, walk through the park, or go to the gym at my leisure. It's become a pleasure and not a chore. I've learned to really enjoy my food, too. I still eat very healthy but it's outside the scope of being a vegetarian and I have no problem indulging in a glass of red wine. My day-to-day is not a fraction as hectic as it was, and I've created time to pursue projects and hobbies that bring me fulfillment. I also stopped dating as an assignment and feel really good about where I am in my personal life.

I truly believe that I had it all wrong before and my body acting out physically was a wake-up call. Being healthy isn't just a measure of how far you can run, how flexible you are, or how defined your six pack is. You want to feel well and be physically fit but not neglect the importance of things like love, friendship, happiness, community, creativity, and having fun.

Those are the things that will carry you through life and make it worth living.

five

Body by Design

In the 1987 film, *The Princess Bride,* there's a scene in which Prince Humperdinck is lamenting that he's swamped because he has to plan his country's 500th anniversary, arrange his marriage, murder his wife and frame a rival kingdom for her death. "Get some rest," advises Count Rugen. "If you haven't got your health, then you haven't got anything."

While the latter is a funny line because of its tongue-in-cheek delivery and context, the saying itself couldn't be more true. No matter how challenging our situation is, we can often work through it if we have good health. If, for instance, we're in a financial crisis, we can work a couple of jobs. If we have young children, we have the strength to chase them around. If we need to make important decisions where people are counting on us, our minds are sharp.

That said, why then do we abuse our bodies so much and, in doing so, sabotage our energy and emotional well being?

The following situations aren't from my personal experience but reflect oft-repeated sequences of events told to me by clients and friends.

Scenario A

Throughout your childhood you are pretty much carefree. You don't pay too much attention to what you eat unless you have a weight issue. In college you find yourself partying every other night, drinking, then having the "go to" 2 a.m. slice of pizza and putting on what's known as the Freshman 15.

Post college you move into a more stable life professionally, but since you're only in your 20's you still have the energy to go out all the time. Dinners and drinks with friends, clubbing, and even hooking up more than you'd like to admit happens because you're in environments that lead to casual sex. As you start to sober up and replay the night's previous events, you're mortified by your behavior and feel depressed across the board for your actions.

By the time you hit your 30's, you start to feel it a little more, you need more sleep and the alcohol wakes you up during the night. You start to limit your partying to 2-3 days a week unless you're married with kids. You advance in your career, your hours are more intense; this means less time for exercise. The stress is beginning to build. You also become more mature and cautious about sexual partners and are probably hiding those Mardi Gras beads deep in your closet. What once seemed like fun is now causing serious havoc in your life. If you eat or drink without caution, there are going to be consequences. Similarly, being physically intimate without caution can be emotionally wounding down the road. Both behaviors that previously never always conjured a second thought have begun planting the seeds for long-term damage.

Whether you find yourself struggling with exhaustion, depression, anxiety, being overweight or having low self-esteem, a lot of these behaviors are a result of not taking better care of your body. To cope with the instability of life, you don't have time to slow down and so instead you resort to prescription drugs. Whether it's uppers or downers, something is needed to take the edge off. You tell yourself it's only temporary but it's only a matter of time before you're totally hooked.

Your body isn't what you had hoped for. You beat yourself up for not being skinny enough or perfect enough. You're not married and feel like you're competing with the dating pool that's 10 years younger. You try juice cleanses or extreme diets that maybe help you drop a pound or two of water weight, but in a week you feel defeated, say "screw it" and go back to the way you've always eaten. You want to get to the gym after work but Happy Hour seems like the more logical option because that's what everyone else is doing. You succumb to the peer pressure and, before you know it, it's 9 p.m. by the time you finally get home. You're buzzed from the two martinis or glasses of wine and the last thing you're craving is a salad. You think "Some Italian sounds amazing right about now" and go for the pasta and garlic bread. You get on your couch and watch the last 30 minutes of *The Bachelorette*, then make a few phone calls. It's now 10:30 and you pull out your lap-top to start checking emails. The work stuff is boring you with the state of mind that you're in so you decide to check out Facebook. All the nonsense is endless. When you're tipsy, cyberstalking your ex seems way more interesting. It's now after midnight and you have to be up at 6:30 a.m. to shower, commute, and get to the office on time. You don't feel rested, but have a long day ahead of you. This is your life.

Scenario B

You pride yourself on being responsible. You were always close to your family and have a great community and a supportive network of friends. College wasn't about partying; it was about excelling and get-ting the career you were passionate about. You also knew at a young age you were ready to settle down and have children. Drinking, smok-ing, and staying out late aren't a part of your world, but celebrations - even the ones you're not excited about - are a constant. Whether it's running to kids' birthday parties, Bar Mitzvahs, communions, Shabbat dinners, or Sunday feasts, your calendar is always booked with occa-sions that revolve around eating. Before you know it, you find your-self gaining weight, possibly pre-diabetic, elevated cholesterol, and it's even hard to recognize yourself when you look at photos before having children that are only just a couple years old.

You don't sleep much because you have to get the kids to school and arrive to work on time. With lack of rest, the last thing on your mind is sex and so that becomes less of a priority. One of you is more sexual and feels unfulfilled. You're also not as turned on by your part-ner because in some ways they've let themselves go. You wouldn't con-sider cheating, but the only consolation is to get attention elsewhere.

You take up tennis, Pilates, or working out with a private trainer and flirt with them for some short-term satisfaction. While you're busy getting fit, you're growing more resentful of your partner for being out of shape and lazy. To make matters worse, one of you is on the computer late at night "friending," chatting, or commenting on someone's Facebook photos that you have never seen or met before. Your partner starts to catch on and fears that you're going through a midlife crisis and will soon leave them for a younger, sexier, replacement. Depression kicks in, sometimes leading to prescription medication or just a constant anxiety about instability in the relationship. This is your life.

These two situations are all too familiar although it doesn't have to go down like this. It's easy to blame our external environment for the breakdown of our physical health and emotions. Every day we are faced with decisions and we tend to choose the path of least resistance. We can't just coast - we have to take responsibility for our outcomes. Even at a young age, I didn't get wrapped up in Scenario A because my mother's early death was a wakeup call. I could have easily been pulled into partying every night, eating unhealthy, having multiple sexual partners - but all of that seemed like scary stuff. Even if it meant avoiding certain friends, or being made fun of for being boring, I just didn't care. No one had the power to convince me to abuse my body. Once the party is over, you're on your own and don't want to be listening to the voice of regret.

In the second scenario, even being a parent doesn't mean that you stop living for yourself. Children learn by watching the example set by you. You will always have events and celebrations but your health comes first. Exercise and play with your kids. Buy healthy foods, get them excited about good nutrition, and be selective when eating out. And who says when you turn 30, 40, or 50 that you need to stop being sexy and now look like a mom or dad? Even worse, you don't need to start developing premature health problems that prevent you for being there for the course of their childhood.

The body we live in is by design; we didn't just wake up that way. I've seen people make 360's in their health, but it's comes from a shift in consciousness rather than nutrition alone. Just going gluten free, cutting out sugar, or eating more vegetables isn't going to fix your problems. You have to make yourself number one and realize that today's lifestyle choices will dictate sickness or health later on. As someone who has gone through cancer, it's a no brainer. I will never get lazy about what I eat, my work outs, the amount of sleep I get, my spirituality, and the love and affection that is required in my life.

It's never too late to make a change, but it's dependent on you to not hold anyone accountable but yourself.

six

Age, Attitude and Expectations

While it's sometimes hard to welcome each birthday, I wouldn't trade the person I've ripened into over time for being younger again. Although it wasn't always easy for me to say that. I remember the months leading up to turning 30 and how I believed that if I wasn't married and didn't have enough money saved to not be stressed about all my expenses, I had somehow failed. While so many other people considered me to be a success for a lot of the things I had achieved such as raising myself, having a good head on my shoulders, and being able to afford an apartment in the most expensive city in the country, I was terrified about not meeting the specific expectations on my list regarding love and money. You're not alone if you put pressure on yourself with these landmark birthdays (30, 40, 50 and beyond) to have everything lined up perfectly. We think we're getting old and buy into, "If we don't have what we want now, it's too late."

When age 30 came, I realized I had made a big deal out of nothing. I was also a far cry from being "old." Around that time I had dated a few men that were very eligible bachelors. As I looked into their relationship history, their most serious relationships were, surprisingly, with older women. I loved what one of the men told me which was, "I'm not an ageist." He went on to explain how older women were sexier, better in bed, and that dating 25 year olds was kind of boring. While I was missing being in my 20's because I had assumed that's what men wanted, this new information was refreshing to hear. I now realized there was a pool of super desirable men who were looking for women that had life experience, opinions, and in their 30's - just like me.

I also had the impression that most men believed that once a woman exited her 20's or even early 30's, she was past child-bearing age. Nowadays, if a man feels that way I know he's foolish. I have a very close girlfriend that had her first child at 50!

It's understandable if you want to have a family that you and your partner start the planning for it early on. Thinking back, though, I realize how young I was when I first decided to marry. As mature as I thought I was compared to my peers, I still didn't really know myself. (It's one of the main reasons why that relationship didn't last very long.) Now if a 25 year old like me who had already been living on her own almost nine years in a Manhattan wasn't ready to be a wife, just imagine how poorly prepared a young lady is that has just left her parents' home or college dorm to get married. Book smarts don't translate into emotional intelligence - that comes with age and experience.

* * *

The rules of aging are changing and I'm not the only one that thinks most of today's most gorgeous actresses are not in their 20's but in their 40's. Jennifer Aniston, J Lo, Gwyneth Paltrow, Sophia Vergara, Salma Hayek, Catherine Zeta-Jones, Halle Berry, Cate Blanchett, Nicole Kidman, Naomi Watts, Elizabeth Hurley, Uma Thurman, Jennifer Connelly, Rachel Weisz, Amanda Peet, and Kate Beckinsale are by no stretch of the imagination cougars. I don't think there is a man on earth that would kick any of those women out of bed!

Not only are those women physical beauties but their elegance, sophistication, sensitivity, confidence, and warmth shine through both onscreen and off. This is the true essence of a woman that makes herself alluring beyond perky boobs and a bubbly personality. A man who is only looking for a pretty young thing is probably not the best candidate to strive for. Even if you meet his criteria, it's likely down the road he'll trade you in for a younger model.

When I see middle-aged women scandalously dressed on the prowl to compete with women 20 years younger, I don't know why they do it to themselves. What they're sending out is a message that says, "Look at me! I'm only worth my value in hotness!" Contrast this to women who are 50 years or older and who project age-appropriate style and self-assurance. I love checking out the chic women on the way to temple on the Sabbath or headed to church in their Sunday best wearing tailored skirt suits and beautiful hats. They're dressed modestly but with so much class, not a desperate scream for attention and validation. They're a reminder of what it means to be a lady - an aspiration that, sadly, seems to be diminishing with each successive generation.

It has long been said, of course, that men age differently than women and yet still engage in similar attempts of vanity to hang on to their youth with a vise-like grip. Instead of freaking out about getting older and having a midlife crisis, a man should embrace his age, chill out, and take pride in his decades of accomplishment. Listen up, guys: Trying to pull off being a playboy in your fifties isn't going to fool anyone, much less make any woman want to be with you. If you look like Pierce Brosnan – now 60 – why are you trying so hard to project Zac Efron? Not only is a mature man "seasoned" – and recognizes that salt and pepper hair and expression lines can be sexy – but the right wardrobe also speaks volumes about his confidence. A button-down shirt with jeans or slacks, for instance, is much more appealing than a deep V-neck with grey chest hair, a fake tan and Botox.

* * *

Why is it that there are some parts of the world – particularly the Mediterranean and the Orient - where the local denizens live measurably longer lives than anyone else? In 2005, author/explorer/researcher Dan Buettner advanced the concept of "Blue Zones" (so named for the blue pen he used to circle target regions) and suggested that cultural, environmental, dietary and spiritual practices are contributing factors to extraordinary longevity. Do these elements hold the secret to the fountain of youth? Buettner's demographic findings based on the following common denominators make a strong argument to that effect:

- **Find your purpose**. When you wake up in the morning, create something meaningful to do or work towards.
- **Have faith**. It doesn't matter if you pray to God, Buddah, Allah, or The Universe, knowing that you have some divine help will get you through the toughest of times.
- **Love and community**. Keep family and loved ones close by for support and guidance.
- **Stay social**. A social life with healthy behaviors will keep your mind and body active.
- **Relax**. Don't underestimate the importance of downtime. Rest, pray, meditate, and do things that don't create stress.
- **Move naturally**. Pumping iron, triathlons, and no pain/no gain mentality are American hobbies. Garden, take a walk or ride your bike outdoors in nature.
- **Eat less**. Eat slowly and stop when you are about 80 percent full. We have a limited amount of enzymes to break down the foods we eat. Eating smaller quantities helps to use fewer enzymes, therefore, prolonging life.
- **Stay away from processed foods**. The food in the Mediterranean and Japan is not tainted like in the United States. GMO foods are widely cautioned against. The food you buy at the market during the day is then cooked for dinner, not kept in the freezer for weeks.
- **Drink Wine**. While alcohol has a bad rap, red wine has antioxidants, polyphenols and flavonoids that are very beneficial for the heart.

So how many practices on that list do you follow? Do you take care of your physical body and spirit or live a stressed existence without enough time in the day, surrounded by the wrong people with not enough emphasis on your own well being? The more stressed and unfulfilled we feel, the more it shows in our appearance. Without slowing down, there isn't time to cook healthy, exercise, and do prayer or meditation.

When I find myself overworked, stressed, cranky, and the bus driver calls me M'am instead of Miss, I know it's time for a break. I will get out of the city, my usual escape route being Florida. I have such a strong network of supportive friends there that I'm closer to than my actual family. I make sure to get at least 15-30 minutes of sun everyday which feels better than anything. I sleep uninterrupted from the sounds of the city traffic that I usually deal with all hours of the night. I eat early and – because I don't have anywhere to be – I never rush through a meal. Even when I'm in Miami, I avoid the South Beach scene at all costs and just enjoy nature and the beach. Being in a good environment makes me free of anxiety; all of my bodily functions relax and seem to work perfectly, even if I just had weeks of not feeling well at home. After a few days of decompressing, I tend to meet people at the pool who will ask me if I'm visiting on break from school. My look literally changes from a professional thirtysomething woman to a college student. That's how powerful taking care of yourself is.

It also gets back to whether, ultimately, you look at your age as a number (over which you have no control) or as an attitude (which you most certainly can change any hour of the day or day of the week). I've known people who are "old" in their 20's. On the flip side, I've been inspired by – and privileged to know – men and women in their 80's who can literally run circles around people who aren't even half their age.

And, yes, while it's easy to be nostalgic and to even long for the past, you still have the rest of life's journey ahead of you. You're only as old as you think, but wanting to feel young enough to create new and exciting experiences is a dynamic that can occur at any age…and does.

seven

Deal With Your Emotions – or Your Body Will

When we have a disagreement with someone or something unfortunate happens, it's easy to be either totally reactive and freak out or do the opposite and entirely shut down. For a second, think about those people who pushed your buttons or the disappointment you felt when the negative event occurred and how you handled it. It's important to consider the scenarios below.

- If another person was involved- did you address the situation properly and try to see it from their perspective?
- Did you become a victim?
- Did you ignore the situation in the hope it would just go away on its own?
- Are you holding an eternal grudge?

I was never the type to let someone have it or curse them out even if they deserved it. If anything, I would cut that person off and they would become dead to me. That was an even harsher process because I didn't understand the concept of forgiveness. Instead I knew how to shut down and silently punish whoever hurt me. I appeared to others as very calm and level-headed because I hardly raised my voice or stressed over situations that upset me. I believed it was all the yoga that was teaching me how to be in control.

The truth, though, is that I was no better about controlling my anger than the guy who screams at the cab driver for cutting him off on the road. I wasn't so evolved that things didn't get to me; I just did a much better job of suppressing it.

Anger can be a very dangerous emotion. It literally leads to sabotage on all levels. Either we kill relationships by responding out of inappropriate anger or we slowly kill ourselves by holding it in. Our physical body and the functioning of our organs are directly linked to our emotions. We have seven energy centers called "chakras" that explain this process.

1. Root Chakra – The first chakra relates to feeling grounded, stable, and attuned to basic survival. Feelings of fear, uncertainty, and being an outsider can cause blockages in this area. Being over-stimulated can lead to imbalance in the adrenals and kidneys.

2. Sacral Chakra – The second chakra governs our sexuality, intimacy, and creativity. Shutting down or experiencing trauma in these areas can lead to blockages in your reproductive system, menstrual cycles, or the ability to conceive.

3. Naval Chakra – The third chakra is about self-confidence, self-esteem and issues of anger. When you are feeling weak and insecure, you may experience digestive problems, gall stones, or even an ulcer.

4. Heart Chakra – The fourth chakra is about being compassionate, friendly, and warm. It governs intuition and love. When you are closed here, you can be blocked in your heart, chest, and breasts. Have you ever heard of an elderly person who died of a broken heart because they lost their spouse? It's possible…

5. Throat Chakra - This fifth chakra is connected to expressing yourself. When you are too shy or don't say what you need to, you may experience neck, throat, and thyroid problems.

6. Third Eye Chakra – The sixth chakra is related to our intuitive nature. When you are meditating, you connect to this chakra by closing your eyes and focusing on this area. Third eye chakra is connected to the pituitary gland, eyes, head, and lower brain. When someone is deficient or blocked, they are unable to visualize or listen to their intuition.

7. Crown Chakra - The seventh chakra is about wisdom; if you are activated here, you are very aware spiritually. The crown chakra is connected to the pineal gland and upper brain. When you're deficient in this area, you may be skeptical, cynical, apathetic, and much more connected to the material world over the spiritual realm.

Once I began to understand the mind/body connection, many health issues I experienced or witnessed in other people made even more sense. Due to the inability to hear other people out or express myself properly, I was shutting down my throat chakra. I don't think it's a coincidence that the area I had cancer in was in exactly the corresponding organ - my thyroid gland.

My mother experienced much emotional pain from her divorce with my father at such a young age. Her father left her as a little girl and the imprint she had from men caused her heart to shut down. Trying to pay the bills alone while having to support me was extremely difficult. She still dated to find someone to help her raise me. Her second marriage, however, was loveless. Her cancer was in her breasts, which is related to the heart chakra.

Illness often comes from not dealing with our emotions properly. This is literally when the body is in "dis-ease." That's why you hear about people making miraculous recoveries when they watch funny movies, say positive affirmations, or visualize good health. Sometimes it takes these dire situations to realize the importance of implementing these practices.

It's crucial to be aware of how we are handing our challenges. Our health - believe it or not - depends on it. People who know how distressed I grew up would often say, "How are you so normal?" Well, even with my perceived groundedness and together mental state, my imbalance eventually showed up physically. Suppressed emotions need to be dealt with because it's impossible to outsmart the body's natural intelligence!

* * *

You can often see what's happening in someone's life just by looking at them. Perhaps someone has postural defects and they're hunched over because they are carrying a heavy burden. Maybe they are prematurely graying or they are aging much more quickly than they should be. Do they carry extra weight to hide from the world? Or do they feel frail and depressed which causes them to be extremely underweight? When I am working with a new client, my first question isn't, "What do you eat every day?" My first question is, "Are you happy?"

The first step to working on this is to be honest with yourself. What is your issue that you haven't dealt with? I know personally I had a lot of resentment towards my father and all of the relatives on his side whom I felt abandoned by after my mother's death. I was on a mission to show them how I was a great success when I left to live on my own at 16. You know the saying, though: "Resentment is like taking poison and expecting the other person to suffer."

I never really spent time in therapy to talk this out. I tried for a few visits but I was so good at speaking the same psychotherapy babble and analyzing myself in sessions to whomever was counseling me that I took out all the work for them; consequently, they just sat there, agreed, and completely validated my feelings. We never made any progress and I found it boring.

I was then recommended to do a course at The Landmark Forum. This is a 3 day weekend self-development workshop that helps you sort out your past. For about 12 hours each day, you sit in a huge room with hundreds of total strangers and share your life story. What I took away was:

1. There's the truth about what actually happened to us, and then there's our perception of what occurred.

2. We put too much meaning into what actually happened. For example, if my father left or a relative was absent, it wasn't about me; it was their own issue. I stopped taking it personally. This helped clear up some of my abandonment issues.

3. Complaining is unproductive. If you keep complaining and not making changes, you will keep experiencing the same issues.

4. Forgive people from your past. Now I don't know if it's always a good idea to contact friends or relatives from 20 years ago, but when you let the anger and resentment go I can see how this can be therapeutic.

Shortly after taking this course, my paternal grandfather passed away. At that time I was out of touch with him because I found him to be mean and even felt a little scared of him. Nor was I in touch with any of his relatives, including my own father. I heard the news through an aunt I didn't particularly have a good relationship with that the funeral was taking place in Florida. So here was my opportunity to apply what I had just learned. I decided to fly down to pay my respects and be surrounded by the evil clan of family members (that's how I previously saw them) and make peace.

After the funeral, the family was sitting Shiva at my grandfather's home. This is the Jewish mourning period of seven days following the burial. I felt really uncomfortable to talk to anyone but I also knew this wasn't the time to be insensitive. Since everyone was feeling sad, I knew they were humbled and possibly willing to put things in the past. I asked each relative I was angry with to sit in my grandfather's room so we could clear the air. Without getting into petty details of why things happened between each one of us, I just said, "I know you didn't mean to hurt me and I hope we can put our differences behind us." I wished them well with sincerity. Maybe it was also a bit of a selfish act because I felt so much better afterwards.

Who wants to live life with enemies feeling like you have an evil eye upon you? It's much better to release those emotions because they will never serve you. You're not foolish or naïve to be able to forgive. A teacher of mine once quoted an expression that goes "Dark mind bitter body." As difficult as it is- letting go with an open heart can be the best medicine for a long life.

eight

No One's Perfect

As the lyrics to *New York, New York* go, "If I can make it there, I'll make it anywhere." Manhattan is a tough city to survive in on so many levels. We have some of the smartest, richest, most beautiful, most successful, and most arrogant people on the planet living here. You feel like you're constantly competing to have the most prestigious job with the biggest bank account, the best clothes, the coolest social life, the largest list of contacts, and the most desirable partner or spouse.

The truth is, everyone is flawed…and everything is spin. Even famous people we admire, emulate, and envy all come with their own set of issues. What is outwardly shown to the world is very different from what exists behind closed doors. In my Wellness business, I've worked with many clients and observed that the raging anxiety levels and insecurities are oftentimes the worst with overachievers who appear to have everything going for them.

Do you honestly think there are human beings that don't experience some level of self-doubt, don't make mistakes, never have morning breath, fart, or have poop that smells? Are you embarrassed because you haven't achieved the financial dreams you hoped for or, through misfortune, lost everything you had? Are you divorced or have several failed relationships under your belt? Were there times you didn't feel like you were worthy of someone or something because if they found out "the truth" about you, you wouldn't be accepted? It might help to remind yourself that even our heroes may have experienced and overcome the same problems as you.

One of the things I've always been complimented on is my calm and grounded demeanor. Ironically, I was a bottle of anxiety from my constant disappointments and uncertainty over the years. I kept cool on the outside, but on the inside it had manifested into a serious nervous stomach. When something of importance was at stake such as a relationship or having to perform, my symptoms would be the worst. Many times it would take me forever to leave my apartment – specifically, my bathroom - if I knew I was walking into these situations. Let's just say that this condition made me feel anything but perfect. I learned how to become very sneaky about this embarrassing problem.

I remember the first boyfriend I was too uncomfortable to open up to about my spastic colon out of fear he would no longer be attracted to me. This guy lived on the Upper East Side and his apartment was around the corner from The Bloomingdales Flagship store on 59th street. My stomach would be the worst in the morning and I was so self-conscious about my issue that I kept it hidden from him and, subsequently, from every relationship after. While he thinks I'm this hot girlfriend that he just had a steamy night with, I would have rather died than blow up his bathroom and spoil the fantasy. Now to be clear, we were not talking about a stranger. This was someone I had dated for months. Instead of snuggling after waking up, there were times I would run out abruptly to say I was getting coffee and then go to the department store to use the bathroom. I made plenty of guys think something was wrong with them when, in fact, it was 100% my issue.

I was curious to know if I was alone with my problem so I began searching online. I found out my experience wasn't so uncommon. I discovered there were lots of celebrities that were not quite as perfect as I had imagined. Many of these people were surprisingly very open about their personal issues. Not that I wished my problems on anyone else but I felt some comfort after discovering who else struggled with embarrassing digestive issues:

- John F. Kennedy
- "Wonder Woman" Linda Carter
- Shannon Doherty
- Tyra Banks

- Kurt Cobain
- Jenny McCarthy

While masking my own stuff, I had become the "Go To" for every-one else's health problems, life problems, etc. I'd see all kinds of imbalance from all these seemingly perfect people. Whether it was cancer, diabetes, digestive problems, an unattractive skin condition, addiction, or financial stress, the common theme would be guilt or embarrassment.

Even one of the hottest women on the planet, Angelina Jolie, had the hereditary cancer gene and decided to undergo a preventative double mastectomy.

The following sexy stars all had cancer- not to mention we can also add that one to my own checklist of imperfections:

- Christina Applegate (breast cancer)
- Brooke Burke (thyroid cancer)
- Sophia Vergara (thyroid cancer)
- Cheryl Crow (breast cancer)
- Rod Stewart (thyroid cancer)
- Michael Douglas (throat cancer)

Having a skin condition is not easy even in the normal world, but imagine if you are constantly being photographed or on camera like these divas with psoriasis:

- Kim Kardashian
- LeAnn Rimes

The list doesn't end there…

- Lady Gaga - borderline lupus
- Lil Wayne - epilepsy
- Montel Williams - Multiple Sclerosis
- Michael J. Fox - Parkinson's disease
- Toni Braxton - lupus and heart disease
- Prince - epilepsy
- Brett Michaels - diabetes and heart disease

Not everyone will have health issues, but it's a part of life for everyone to have setbacks. If you think someone has it all because they're wealthy, remember that money can also disappear in an instant. Look at the Lehman Brothers' collapse, the instability of the stock market, and the Bernie Madoff scam. I've seen friends and clients that had their 15 minutes of fame but couldn't handle their new fortune and lost it all. On the flip side, think of all the stories of people who had nothing and - through motivation and persistence - became mega rich.

These celebrities went through a low point where they didn't have a traditional roof over their head - whether it was living in a car, homeless shelter, or on the street:

- Jewel
- Tyler Perry
- Dr. Phil
- Shania Twain
- William Shatner
- "Rocky" Sylvester Stallone
- Halle Berry
- Celebrity Stylist Paul Mitchell

The bottom line is this: Don't beat yourself up for what you consider to be a flaw. If handled the right way, these "imperfections" make us better, stronger, and more humble individuals. They also teach us important life skills like empathy and can be used as a way to weed out the people who don't belong in your life. If you think a potential friendship or relationship is at stake because you are going to be judged, do you really want that stress? Keep in mind that we are a mirror for other people. Whatever someone criticizes or feels deeply bothered about in you is really something that they need to work on in themselves.

nine

A Leopard Can Change its Spots

The phrase "B'Kiso, B'Kaso, B'Koso" is a statement of wisdom from the Jewish sages. They explain that there are three ways in which one can find out the true character of another person: B'Kiso (With his wallet), B'Kaso (With his temper), or B'Koso (when he's drunk). Although it's spoken about in the context of men, this also applies to women. Under pressure, stress, difficulty, and upheaval, you can get to see someone's true nature a lot more quickly. Does that person become defensive, lose control or act out when challenged? Without a frame of reference – such as knowing someone for a long time – it's sometimes hard to assess whether these behaviors are a triggered – and temporary - response to extenuating circumstances or a deeply ingrained facet of his/her personality. That said, I tend to be fairer than most in that I try to give people another chance.

There's another well known expression - "There are no atheists in fox holes" - that was said to have originated with a Christian chaplain in the U.S. Army during World War 11. Even the most cynical person that never had any faith may reconsider his or her belief systems and start praying during life-threatening times and moments of desperation.

It's easy to find fault with others and to be extremely critical when it comes to their poor judgment, differences, or imperfections. While there are always going to be a few bad eggs, there are also people with kind hearts whose behaviors have been negatively influenced by unfortunate circumstances, surroundings, and their peers.

When I used to practice yoga every day at 6 a.m. in Soho, I would look around the room and see quite a few male students with long hair tatted up looking like Axl Rose. Now I know there had to be a story why guys who could pass for Guns N' Roses band members would want to be doing yoga at the crack of dawn on a Sunday morning. I jokingly wondered whether they had just come from doing a gig at CBGB's, a place where punk rockers performed on the Lower East Side. Even though I have bad celebrity radar, I heard that some of these guys actually were famous rock stars or were in 90's heavy metal bands. I guess for whatever reason maybe they were sober or just over their partying days and were now focusing on their inner selves.

Have you ever heard of a rock star that didn't ever party, do drugs, and have a lot of sex? Does that mean they're bad people because they were once out of control? They all have crazy stories – some of which are glorified as part of their edgy image and others that they may not be so proud of. When you have an addictive personality or live/work in an environment that breeds temptation, it can make you act in ways that you didn't even know you were capable of.

It's almost impossible to go cold turkey on destructive behavior unless you find another way to channel your energy along with a good support system. This is why many people who went wild in their heyday will take that fire for excitement and novelty and subsequently turn to religion or spirituality. This isn't necessarily a bad thing; in fact, if they stay on track and commit to their newfound goals, it's totally admirable.

With struggle comes maturity, and some of the wisest people are guilty of at one point having done some pretty reckless things. It's a lot harder for individuals to turn their lives around and now make the right choices when their inclination is pushing them the other direction. For someone who grew up sheltered and never went off-course, they may appear to be the "better" person…but are they really? They're just doing what they have always known and it didn't require any work on themselves.

In friendships, relationships, and even when seeking advice, I want to hear the perspective of people who weren't always so perfect, took risks, and definitely turned their lives around and learned from their mistakes. Sometimes we have to go through pain, embarrassment, and major disappointments to be humbled enough to make a change in our character.

* * *

If it wasn't for my childhood, I'm sure I'd be a lot different. After my mother's death, my father's absence and bouncing around to different schools, I had a major chip on my shoulder. I had aggression towards anyone that was spoiled, had both parents, and seemed not to have any problems. I was always ready for a fight; whether it was physical or verbal, I wanted to show that this skinny white girl had "street cred" from growing up on her own. Along with that attitude came aloofness, apathy, and a judgmental streak against anyone who seemed the slightest bit weak.

Since I always knew right from wrong, I wasn't about to steal or do drugs as a way of acting out. I did, however, have the same problems or even worse than many of the inner city kids and minorities. I was drawn to hanging out with bad boys and dated a guy from a nearby rough neighborhood in Queens. He was a complete hoodlum. Many nights hanging out with him and his friends would be at empty handball or basketball courts watching them drink forties, smoke blunts, listen to rap music, and act like total misfits. If I have a daughter someday who dates this kind of guy and pulls these same moves, I'll ground her for life!

The aunt and uncle I was living with weren't so happy either but this was part of my rebellion. I hated living with them and since this guy was older and had a basement apartment in his parent's house, I was able to sleep there often and escape. During this time, my mother's childhood friend, Beverly, would call me every night from Florida where she was living. She was scared about the road I was going down and what would become of me. She was a single mom with two boys around my age and thought it would be a good idea to get away from New York and this scenario for a bit. I knew in my gut this wasn't the life I wanted. Sad as I was about leaving New York, I knew it was the right decision to say "yes" when she invited me to come and live with her.

When I got there I had to get acclimated to a school curriculum that was totally different. Although I was bright and a former honor's student, my mind was shut down. I would have homework and book reports and couldn't concentrate. I was unable to read and retain anything and felt so frustrated. Beverly was extremely understanding and patient because she was a therapist and had been a nursery school teacher. We would sit in bed together and she would read to me like I was a child. I felt ashamed at times and wanted to cry. She would also talk to me about everything and anything so I wouldn't keep my emotions trapped. I had blocked out so many memories as a way to cope with all the trauma.

I came to her as a wounded bird and, within six months, her influence - along with her two sons that I came to love like brothers - gave me incredible healing. They were my angels and in just that short amount of time I was redirected on another path. After our time together, I moved back to New York, but this go-round was much more focused. I was now with a roommate and, being that I was underage and was afraid to get caught, I had to stay out of trouble. I never spoke to the old boyfriend again or anyone in those circles.

If I look at who I am now as opposed to where I was headed then, it seems like another life. Where would I have ended up professionally? Would I have become a teenage parent, then trying to discipline kids that were total thugs? People I meet these days often assume I was private schooled in Manhattan by wealthy parents. No one in my current circles would ever believe I was the same person. I have so much gratitude because I realize how lucky I was to be loved and redirected. Beverly didn't give up on me and still plays a major role in my life.

When you care for someone and see their potential, don't always be quick to abandon them if they take a couple of wrong turns. Everything is not so black and white and not everyone is afforded the same opportunities that you may have had. On the flipside, their opportunities may have been a breeding ground for mayhem. Without judgment, try to put yourself in their shoes. Sometimes that very person's situation is put in our path not just for that individual to change but for us to grow by helping them.

ten

Daddy Issues

With all the issues surrounding male figures in my life, without faith I could have completely written off the potential for love.

The first man who unintentionally let me down was my father. My parents had a rocky marriage and they divorced by the time I was six years old. My father was the irresponsible, fun one and my mother was the disciplinarian. She maintained full custody after they split up but my father would occasionally pick me up for the day on weekends. I remember things like going to carnivals, eating candy, and seeing movies with him. They were generally bloody martial arts films or comedies that I had no business watching, especially before I was even a teenager. One of my memories was going to the movie *I'm Gonna Git You Sucka.* It was a one of Chris Rock's first movies and also starred the Wayans brothers. I still remember funny details such as a pimp who wore giant platform shoes with live goldfish in the heels.

My dad liked to visit movie theatres that were located in dangerous neighborhoods because there were mostly minorities. He thought it was hysterical when big black women would "talk to the screen." He actually wasn't racist at all, but most of the time he was stoned and would find humor in the stupidest things.

His inappropriateness didn't end with the activities he chose for us. He worked as a pharmaceutical rep but, ironically, not everything he pushed needed a prescription; he also sold pot. I've never been a smoker but I do recall from watching him how to roll my first joint by the time I was eight years old. Some visiting days he would pick me up, have me sit in the backseat, and invite one of his clients to sit up front to test out the marijuana quality. They would fog up the car with me in it.

I still loved him despite the pot - and sometimes harder drugs - that would sneakily be used in my presence. It was also unfortunate that the neighbors knew about his recreational habits. For a few years he lived in a house that had the windows taped from all the break-ins; I would be scared to spend the night there. He was usually low on money and my mother would complain that he didn't pay child support. He started to come around less and less and I hardly saw him anymore.

The thing about my father was that he wasn't a mean guy, nor was he ever critical or abusive in any way. He was actually kind of apathetic and so consumed with himself that he wasn't the kind of dad who would help with homework, offer advice, or ask how I was coping with my mother's illness. He wanted me to figure my stuff out and not have to rely on him for anything.

It was upsetting when he disappeared on me because, in many ways, he was my outlet. Even though his behavior and lack of disciplining may have been viewed as off-the-wall by others, I always laughed so much around him. He would put underwear on his head to be funny or dance around the apartment like an idiot. He wanted to be a comedian at one point and I remember him sitting in his bedroom with a tape recorder listening to himself tell stories. I never really paid attention to what he was saying but whenever I walked by and knew what he was doing, I felt like I wanted to pee in my pants. I definitely have a serious side, but there are times when my inner goofball is unleashed and I know it's because of him.

* * *

My stepfather, on the other hand, was very different. He was much more involved in my life but seemed to be disapproving of everything I did. He had a serious temper, constantly insulted me, and instilled tremendous fear not only in me but also my mother. He lacked any sense of lightness which was what my biological father was all about.

He would always scream at her and even say things like, "Why don't you just die already!" With his beady eyes and thick, black moustache, I used to call him Hitler. There were even times that he would drink and call up my sexy 13-year-old girlfriend with the blonde hair and big boobs to flirt with her. I was always uncomfortable being alone in the house with him on the all-too frequent occasions my mom was in the hospital. He said some off color things to me when he was drunk, although I was relieved that he never crossed the line.

My mother grew to hate him but when you have terminal cancer and a child to care for, it's not like you can just pack up and leave.

* * *

As I approached my teenage years, I was out of touch with both my father and stepfather. My mother was gone and I didn't have any men who protected me. From fear of not being loved, I got in a serious relationship with a young man I definitely didn't belong with and yet subsequently married. In many ways, we identified with each other. He had a lot of his own issues and insecurities that made me feel comfortable revealing my own weaknesses. I knew he wouldn't judge me for having a crazy, unstable childhood. He told me that he loved me all the time, called me throughout the day to the point it was smothering, but I felt comfortable in knowing he was loyal and never leave me.

One of the things that originally attracted him was that I was very much a free spirit and loved learning and doing things that brought me happiness. He asked me in the beginning of our relationship if I had plans to take off and go to India to study with my yoga guru. It was actually on my list but I became so addicted to the sense of security with him that I decided not to leave.

Once we became serious, the activities and interests that originally intrigued him had now become threats. My happy and light disposition turned to heavy and depressed. I made a good living as a yoga instructor and massage therapist but when it became obvious he couldn't handle that I had male clients, I eventually quit. I also loved to dance but because of his sobriety he couldn't be in an environment such as a night club where there was alcohol. I wanted to include him in my world so I invited him to attend evening classes and lectures with me but he preferred to stay home and watch sports. If I went alone, he would say that it was just a singles scene and get angry with me for leaving him at home and talking to other guys. He had a temper and I felt like every move I made was the wrong one. His jealousy got much worse in time and caused me to feel like I was always walking on eggshells. One day he found a pair of old boots he couldn't remember he owned and accused me of having another man over.

Finally, I'd had enough. Having a man in my life was not worth the expense of losing my identity. I left him, a decision that literally caused me to lose all of my financial security. I was in a panic and didn't know where to go. I stayed with friends for a few weeks until I figured out who to borrow from in order to be able to put a security deposit on an apartment and pay first and last month's rent.

My girlfriend Barbara came through with an amazing deal. Her great aunt was living in an area of Manhattan called Stuyvesant Town. She lived in a complex that were once projects but were now transitioning into luxury apartments. The fantastic thing about these residences was their size. Most New York apartments are tiny but these were tremendous. Her aunt's two-bedroom apartment had not yet been renovated because she had been there for probably 40 years and didn't want the rent to be quadrupled. When she finally became incapable of taking care of herself, she was moved to assisted living but their family kept the apartment and offered it to me for an unheard-of-price.

Too bad there was a catch. The apartment smelled of mildew that was growing on carpets that hadn't been ripped out since the 70's. The ugly floral print couches were no better. One of the bedrooms was just a storage area for all the grandma paraphernalia – a wheelchair, some old house robes, and photos, etc. There was a bed in there but I was kind of creeped out to sleep on it.

The second bedroom had nothing in it and I didn't have money for a new bed. I took the train to Brooklyn to visit Target and buy a cheap inflatable bed which I then schlepped back to the city. I remember my first night sleeping on the floor. The bed kept deflating and I was all alone but I still felt happier with the freedom to not have to answer to anyone.

I was 28 years old and felt pretty confident that I would start dating again soon, meet someone new, and shortly thereafter get remarried without a problem. It didn't work out like that, though.

While I had never suffered from anxiety, it began showing up terribly in all my future relationships. I went through a five-year string of subconsciously choosing men who were fun, exciting, maybe even dangerous, but definitely not good for me. I had also forgotten how to be ME. Where was the old Danielle who would always speak her mind, never put up with someone's bullshit, and never apologize for not being perfect? I was paralyzed in every relationship and not fully capable of being myself, constantly feeling that if I let go and showed love and vulnerability, I would lose them. Instead, my distance came through and I eventually pushed everyone away.

After replaying the same scenario of failed relationships over and over, I realized I was never going to have a soul partner, a family, or be at peace if I continued to stay shut down. More than any material possession, financial success, or personal accomplishment I plan to achieve, I don't feel like I'm expressing my soul's full potential without being able to share love as well as receive it back. So with the risk of getting hurt, I've made a conscious shift to be open, verbal, and put myself out there even when it's uncomfortable. I love the expression "You can't say the wrong thing to the right person." It's become my motto these days...

eleven

Don't Lose Yourself for a Partner

It's a jungle out there. It seems like every other person I meet is single and the competition is fierce. Just like me, you may have had a short marriage at a young age and are now divorced. Or perhaps you had a long relationship, your kids are grown, and you are now being replaced by someone half your age

If you venture into the "singles scene" it can be really discouraging. Every woman is dressed sexier and more scandalous than the next, and many of the guys are more metrosexual and polished than a lot of the females that are trying to hook up with them. Add to this the fact that most people aren't being authentic with who they actually are. From the moment you arrive at a party or step through the doors of a club, you're being sized up strictly on what you present on the exterior - your looks, your job, your social status, where you went to school - but not by the REAL you. It's like we feel the need to pretend so we can woo someone enough to fall for us.

I used to think shows like *Sex and the City* were ridiculous. Not so much anymore. As someone who has been sucked into the Manhattan dating culture (and now living it myself), I think the reason the series did so well was because there was a lot of truth to the content. Our existence can be terribly shallow and appearance is everything. It would be awesome if there could be some superhuman lens that would bypass our physical shell, our weight, and our beauty so others could see our soul. If that were to happen, all of the good, kind, worthy people – whether attractive and successful or not – would have no issues finding their soul mates.

* * *

When I was newly single, it was really easy to reemerge into the party scene. I didn't want to go that route, however. I thought I'd have a better chance of finding a quality guy in something that I had genuine interest in and which also had some depth. So as a non-observant person who had just been invited to do a religious fellowship program, it seemed like the change I needed.

The course encompassed what would be a conversion class, the exception being that everyone there was Jewish to start with. Gradually I went from wearing my usual tight jeans, high boots, and miniskirts to dressing with much more modesty. One of the requirements of Orthodox Judaism is to be what's called *Tznius*. It was difficult to dress like this all the time, but out of respect I would wear knee length skirts over pants and try to be covered as much as possible. The reason for this is not to draw attention to oneself in a sexual way.

I also began observing the Sabbath by not working on Saturdays, spending money, driving, using my cell phone, computer, or anything electronic. A part of me liked this way of life because it allowed me to totally shut down for 24 hours every week. In addition, I began keeping kosher. I considered myself to be Orthodox but still modern.

Along with this lifestyle comes the "shidduchim" otherwise known as matchmaking. In my circles, marriage was everything and you almost felt like something was wrong with you if you were single. Thus, I agreed to go through the process of being set up.

It was totally awkward. Every guy was the same. Without even knowing them, it would usually be a lawyer, doctor, banker, from Long Island or Brooklyn with his parents still married, and he for sure went to Jewish day school followed by an Ivy League university. He typically was on the straight path, never partied, did drugs, or had a lot of sex, if any. Most girls he usually dated had a predictable safe job or something corporate, and definitely goody two shoes.

The questions would start spewing out from whoever was my date that night. Our conversations often went something like this:

Him: So where did you grow up?

Me: Um, born in New York, then Florida, then Queens after my mom died, then to Manhattan for the end of high school.

Him: Okay, so you must be close to your father?

Me: No, we really don't have a relationship.

Him: So when did your family move to the city?

Me: Well, actually I moved out on my own at 16.

Him: Did you go to private school?

Me: No, I went to public school.

Him: Hmmm. Interesting. So how did you support yourself?

Me: Um…I worked as a bartender and a model.

Him: Really? At 16 and 17?

Me: Yes, but let's get back to you—

Him: So what did you do after that?

Me: I was a massage therapist and yoga instructor.

Him: Okaaaaay. Well, tell me about your relationships. What are you looking for?

Me: I'm actually divorced but would like to get remarried.

Cue the deafening sound of crickets.

This was always the conversation and it would get so strange. The guy could not put me in a box. I was like some orphan, runaway model/bartender, that later did massage and is now divorced. But I'm Orthodox! Can't these guys have an open mind? Jeez!

I started to realize that no matter how hot I looked on a date, my challah baking skills would be what would really seal the deal. Unfortunately, I had none nor was I a serious cook. Unless you were a health nut like me that also appreciated egg white omelets or a plain grilled piece of fish with steamed vegetables, I wasn't serving up meals like their Jewish mothers.

* * *

Along the way I surprisingly met someone that was from the same Orthodox world but rather than judge me, he seemed intrigued. He was one of 10 children from a Hasidic Jewish background called

Chabad Lubavitch. He actually went by his biblical name Avraham rather than an easier or more modern abbreviation.

I always liked Chabad people because they were much more mystical and warmer than the more conservative Jewish groups, not to mention they treated all Jews like family. I had even been contacted by random Chabad people (married couples with a family) through Facebook who noticed I would sometimes go by my Hebrew name Devorah. As total strangers it was not uncommon to receive a Facebook message with an invite to their home for Shabbat. Sometimes I accepted the invitations and met some really amazing people. I was surprised that these couples were definitely not crazy but, instead, some of the warmest and even most prominent business owners in Manhattan.

Avraham was young - roughly the same age as me - but he was already divorced with three children. Although that part wasn't ideal, I loved that he had such a big family and thought it would be amazing to go from being an only child without having parents to potentially marrying into a family with tons of relatives. I thought maybe I could do this. He was so spiritual, kind, fun, cute, super attentive, and really wanted to get married (unlike most guys in New York). His list of admirable qualities went on and on.

While the idea seemed so romantic, there were a lot of drawbacks. Although he looked modern, he was Ultra Orthodox. That meant I had to wear skirts and keep covered at all times, we could only eat in kosher restaurants, and we could never have a meal at any of my friends' homes that were not Ultra Orthodox as well. (By his rules, my friends' food would not be kosher enough - even if they were Jewish.) Additionally, if we married I would have to cover my hair with a wig or hat. To be fair, I have no judgment about any of this. This is simply the lifestyle of being with someone in this community. It was just so different from the world that I came from; in his world, there could be no such thing as compromising.

As I started to weigh the pros and cons of the situation, I knew I couldn't drag this out. I became filled with anxiety and it was even reminiscent of how I came to marry my ex-husband. He represented security, family, and loyalty - but with that came a lot of control. Now my ex's rules were not for religious reasons but - due to his jealousy - I couldn't dress the way I wanted, I couldn't talk to men, I was removed from close friends because he didn't approve, and I revolved my entire life around fitting into his universe.

How scary! I was not permitted to be myself and do things the way that was comfortable or familiar with either of these guys. I had to completely conform to make both of these relationships work. I felt so trapped and inhibited when I was married that I questioned how can I even entertain going back to that life? Once it clicked for me, I knew what I had to do. I wished Avraham the best but had to say goodbye.

Sometimes the same situation occurs for us several times until we get the lesson. My lesson was not to lose myself in someone else. It was hard to make the connection right away – especially because these two men were seemingly so different - but when I looked closer, it was clear the exact situation would have repeated itself.

It's the best thing in the world to find love but not at the expense of giving up everything. You may get married or even have a child if that's what you so deeply desire but ultimately your soul will feel unfulfilled. Before you jump into something too serious, spend time with this person around your friends and family and observe if they get along. Be open about your core beliefs and aspirations. Make sure they are in alignment or at least respected by your partner. There are some things you can compromise on but never on WHO you are.

twelve

Surround Yourself with Only Positive People

There is a quote that goes, "You are the average of the five people you spend the most time with." The amount of success and happiness we experience is greatly influenced by those we allow in our inner circle. The beginning of any relationship is usually built through trust and intuitive feelings. Whether it's romantic, business related, or just friendship, we tend to gravitate toward people that make us feel good. Still, it's easy to get entangled in negative relationships because it's scary to call someone out on their bad behavior or entirely cut that person out of your life.

If you're afraid of losing friends or a lover that doesn't treat you well, it's likely they will sense your weakness and walk all over you. Do you have people in your life that always take and don't give back? I'm referring to the ones who dump their problems on you but don't ask how your day was, use you for your social connections but don't share their resources with you, or like to date you when it's convenient for them but are not emotionally available when things get serious. This is when the scales are not balanced. It's only gimme gimme gimme, and you are always left feeling short-changed.

If this is happening to you, it's important to take a moment and reflect on why you are putting up with it. Do you feel like people won't like you if you're not constantly pleasing them? Are you afraid of being alone? If your giving of affection is unearned – and yet expected by the other party - you will constantly be taken advantage of. Misery loves company and when you are unhappy, they feel fed. By not putting your foot down, this cycle will repeat itself in all areas of your life.

* * *

We've all experienced friends and relatives who pretend to want the best for us but it comes off as completely phony. Those are often the most dangerous people since we have no clear-cut reason or justification to push them away. They may be polite and exhibit all of the niceties but it's obvious they gain fulfillment by seeing you unhappy. They know how to compliment you at the same time as giving a dig. I would often get this from girlfriends in dating situations. Even though New York seems like a big city, the dating pool can be very small, especially in Jewish circles. Since I'm also very tall, that made the selection even more limited. Let's say there is a top 10 percent of the most eligible guys who had the height, the looks, the charm, etc.; those would be the guys that people would think to set me up with.

Given that this 10 percent was also the most desirable for all the other girls, there would be a fear of scarcity. On the pretense of "It's just because I care about you so much," they were eager to let me know all of the inside gossip about whoever I was dating. In truth, they were really only doing this to make me feel insecure. For example, I'd hear things such as, "You're pretty, but all his ex-girlfriends are much younger" or "You guys will hit it off because he didn't come from money and he won't judge you for how you grew up."

Sometimes they'd see one of my exes out at an event after a break-up and send me a text along the lines of, "Guess who's here, and he's been talking to this girl all night and seems really happy." Even worse were the occasions when a girlfriend would tell me how much an ex was flirting with her or giving her compliments. In my mind, if I've had a break-up with someone, there would be no reason to ruin my Saturday night by running to throw it in my face. It was clear there was so much gratification in hurting my feelings even though it was always set forth under the guise of a so-called good friend looking out for my interests.

After a while I thought, "What is the benefit of allowing this cattiness in my life?" These girls are collectively miserable and if they can't be with anyone, they want you to be alone, too. As I would start getting pulled into their web of negativity, I found myself feeling as unhappy as they were. I began going into dates with a jaded attitude that wasn't even my personality. I was projecting all the belief systems these girls were feeding me onto the guys. What else did I expect? They loved commiserating over the phone each night about how much it sucked to be single and how bad all men are…and made me feel guilty for participating. Having a bad attitude about meeting the right person is obviously not going to attract anyone. I knew I had to get out of that mindset so I decided to cut my ties.

Within a short period of time, it was very freeing to approach dating situations without the input of friends that were projecting their own skewed opinions. I also felt better about the overall experience. Even if I didn't like the guy, I usually ended up having a nice night out and saw the situation for good conversation and meeting someone new. I kept my friends limited to (1) the ones who were married and didn't see me as a threat, and (2) the confident single ones that I knew were rooting for me.

* * *

Beware of people who make you feel small. As someone who grew up on my own without parental influence, my ambitions can sometimes be childlike. When I have an idea that may even sound crazy to other people, I like to go for it. When sharing your ideas, there is such a thing as constructive criticism but don't confuse that with someone else's limitations. A business partner of mine was very superstitious about not discussing our projects with other people. He would say, "You need to imagine yourself as pregnant." In the beginning stages you need to protect the baby or "idea"; otherwise, it won't survive until full term. It needs to be in a safe environment as an embryo so it continues to develop and grow. Then you need to nurture the unborn baby, eat well, feed it, and keep away for dangerous people or situations. The same holds for an idea or business venture you are excited about. By exposing yourself to negative people or situations, they could potentially kill it. The people who are supportive of you will give you love, encouragement, and help give birth to your idea.

I once spoke to a leading astrologer and he explained to me that compatibility in relationships is vibrational. If you are tuned into your surroundings, you may be able to sense a positive or negative vibration coming from someone. If you're sensing negativity from someone – even when they're temporarily saying or doing the right things – it could have to do with their vibration. Sometimes no matter what you do it's impossible to find a way to connect and agree with someone. I am a talkative person, but in certain circumstances I feel like I literally have nothing to contribute to the conversation. This can occur when you and the person are just on completely different wavelengths energetically. Instead of trying to fake a relationship, surround yourself with people that allow you to be open and expressive rather than contracted and afraid to be yourself.

Having a support system of the right people will help you to be the best you can be and to build your confidence when things don't work out. You may also need these people to hold you accountable for your shortcomings. The people closest to you should never leave you feeling anxious, unhappy, or insecure. Instead, they should be your cheerleaders helping you to materialize your dreams.

thirteen

Unexpected Lessons

While it's usually most comfortable spending time with people who are just like you and share the same viewpoints, it doesn't necessarily allow for growth. Many people – including myself at one point - believe that the way they experience things and see the world is the "right" way. Some of my most valuable lessons, however, have come from people who think totally opposite. I've had this happen several times, but the two examples that I'm discussing here have definitely helped me shape my perspective.

My ex-husband was definitely not the typical personality I was used to dating and yet he really gave me tremendous insight into the minds of men. Prior to him, I had mostly gone out with creative types, hipsters, or metrosexuals who had more style than I did. (And I'm pretty sure they were all straight.)

My ex was a regular, down-to-earth, meat and potatoes guy that loved sports. I had never been to a sports bar, played beer pong, or attended a live sporting event aside from Knicks games, which were my exception. I had massage and yoga clients that were professional athletes and got invited all the time to their games, but even with V.I.P. treatment and the best seats in the house, I had no interest. I held on to a judgment that all guys who were crazy about sports were a bunch of meat heads who were loud and obnoxious, spent too much time tailgating, and stuffed their faces with too many hotdogs and beer.

When I met my ex, he worked in sports collectibles and memorabilia. At the time I moved into his apartment I felt like I was moving into the Sports Hall of Fame. Every inch of wall space was covered with autographed Mohamed Ali, Babe Ruth, Sandy Koufax or some old time athlete's photographs. There were signed bobbleheads and baseball gloves on display as if that was his idea of home decor. It definitely clashed with my Moroccan pillows and Shabby Chic furniture that I came with! It bothered me that I saw his choice of hobbies and profession as unsophisticated and unrefined. Looking back, I feel like a total snob - but it goes deeper than that.

I later realized that the subconscious reason I didn't like men who were obsessed with sports was because they reminded me of negative experiences growing up. The jocks from high school weren't nice to me because I was a bit of a loner and the polar opposite of a cheerleader. My stepfather also had a son that played semi-professional baseball and he spent so much of his time at his son's games. His son was the star and to him I seemed untalented or not good at anything.

The more time I spent around my ex, I began to observe how sports represented a way of true bonding for men. There would be times when he wasn't speaking to his father but we were invited over to his parents' place for dinner. When we got to their apartment, there would be a game on television. He and I would sit on the couch across from his parents. Within minutes there would be a foul ball, a lousy pass, or possibly a touchdown. The guys would react to the situation and in no time at all they would be discussing what had just transpired. His mother and I didn't understand the play and had zero to contribute so the two men would start talking. Within minutes they forgot they were even angry with each other.

The other thing I learned about sports was that it has so much value for children. Although I was athletic myself, my abilities didn't develop until I was in my teens. Even then, I wasn't what you'd consider a jock. Kids do much better when they have discipline and something to work towards. It's also a huge factor in cultivating friendships which is something I never had. Trying to take interest in what was important to him, I began following games on television, in the news, and online. It later turned out to be one of the best ways to connect with my male friends, clients and other guys.

* * *

Pietro was only in my life for a season, but I think it had to do with the intensity. Remember the movie *When Harry Met Sally* and they talk about men and women not being able to maintain a friendship? I'd have to agree. Pietro and I became even closer and more intimate as friends than what I had ever experienced in other relationships. Since he was old enough to be my father, I didn't see him in a romantic light but we would talk several times a day about anything and everything. Pietro was Italian, very scruffy, outspoken, foul-mouthed to the point I'd get embarrassed about being in public with him sometimes, but there was truth to most of the things he said. He just didn't care about social etiquette or rules. If you were a jerk, he had no shame in raising his voice and letting you know.

He was also a ladies' man in his time and even dated some of the most beautiful Hollywood actresses in the world. Most of his friends at one point were society's elite or celebrities so it was funny for me to observe him to be so blatant and rough around the edges. On the other hand, I never wanted to be perceived as anything but ladylike. If I'm on a cell phone, I'll always speak softly and cover my mouth when I'm talking. It would totally annoy me to hear someone's entire conversation in a supermarket or on the bus. If someone aggravated me, I'd let them know but very calmly without raising my voice or cursing. So you can imagine how embarrassed I would get around Pietro when he would behave outrageously. I wanted to hide or make up some excuse to abruptly leave him.

Pietro would take his time with everything and move at a snail's pace on purpose. I'm such a New Yorker and everything is a rush, even if I have nowhere to be. I walk fast, I talk fast, and completely lose my patience when people are slow or can't communicate what they need to say in two sentences. When we'd be on the street, he would stop in his tracks to look at every window display, a beautiful woman, or tree that just blossomed. I would freak out and say, "It's rush hour, and we're holding up the foot traffic!" If we were in a store, he felt the need to make friends and chat up every cashier and I'd take his arm and try to drag him out the door.

If you met Pietro just once, you would never forget him whether you loved him or couldn't stand him. He would say, "Danielle, my darling, don't you realize that everyone here is mad? Why are you always running and why do you care so much about what people think about you? So what if you piss someone off for making them wait two seconds."

His outlook made so much sense. I was so desensitized that I'm guilty of having speed-walked right past homeless beggars, would get frustrated when a cashier couldn't ring up my order fast enough, or when commuters didn't run down the subway steps at a quick enough pace and I'd miss my train - even when the next train was only one minute away. There was likewise a sense of feeling sharper, smarter, and more street-smart than everyone else by maintaining my hustle bustle attitude. The question I had to ask myself was, "At what cost?" Was I really getting ahead or improving the quality of my life by being impatient and intolerant, or was I just stressing out my body for nothing?

I also had to reevaluate if my discomfort with Pietros' behavior was really something to be so ashamed of. I started to think that maybe everyone in the world is so wrapped up in their own universe just like I am. It's not like people were even really paying attention to me as a stranger but I chose to always get squeamish about the impression I made in public or things that were truthfully unimportant. Pietros' lessons showed me that life flies by and instead of calmly enjoying it and stopping to smell the roses, we choose to make big deals about nonsense when we don't have to. All my years of studying with spiritual teachers didn't even help that message to sink in. It took an eccentric and very special *Italian* for me to finally get it.

When a person comes into your life that sees the world in a way so against your nature, they are planted there for a reason. If they bother you to a disproportional degree, reflect on whether your reaction stems from insecurity or a past painful or embarrassing experience, then resist the temptation to assume you know better than whomever you are dealing with. Sometimes it's a blow to the ego, but watch how new friends and relationships show up out of nowhere when you change your limited perspective into a place of open mindedness.

fourteen

What You Fear Will Appear

We all know the saying "Be careful what you wish for," but we should also be mindful of thinking too much about things that we hope will never come to fruition. If you know anything about the Law of Attraction, one of the principles is that you'll attract whatever you think about the most - even the bad stuff!

In my case, the one thing I obsessed about during my entire childhood was illness; specifically, cancer. I wasn't even sure if I would live to be older than 38, the age my mother passed. Working in the health field, creating business alliances with doctors, and practicing a holistic lifestyle were all my defenses against the battle of cancer that I was convinced (in my head) I was going to fight against at some point. At the same time, I was preparing myself for the doomsday news; I would pray daily and meditate on not getting cancer. Lo and behold, I was given the report at 30 years old that I did, in fact, have cancer.

Now the question is, was I genetically predisposed to this disease and nature just ran its course? Or by making an affirmative statement to myself that this was coming, did I somehow bring it on? Looking back, my prayers and meditations were not performed in the correct way. Rather than set my intentions on not having cancer, I should have focused on seeing myself healthy and removed the thing I feared most (cancer) from my consciousness entirely.

Once I was actually facing the fear I'd been dreading since I was a child, something strange happened. I never thought about the C word anymore. The scariest thing that had materialized as a result of my thoughts was also a wakeup call. Had my illness only been related to a breakdown in the actual health of my body, I may still have dealt with recurrences or continual problems. Instead, I wiped the fear of cancer from my consciousness and my body made a total shift. It was almost as if the disassociation from the negative thoughts removed me from the universe that cancer lives in.

Although some doctors may say that it was the surgery and radiation that were keeping me healthy, I have to argue that's not fully the case.

* * *

My client, Sarah, was in her mid 30's and desperately wanted a baby. She was in good health and her doctor was not particularly concerned for her. Since some of her other friends around her age were undergoing IVF and having trouble conceiving, however, that became a big fear for her as well.

Even before she and her husband began trying to get pregnant, she imagined there would be problems. It was ironic because her husband is an acupuncturist and fertility specialist. He was always the one that people went to when the traditional course of fertility treatment didn't work. Between the special diet I had her on, nutritional supplements, and the Chinese herbs prescribed by him, it couldn't stand up to her fears and expectations that each pregnancy would be a disappointment.

It was a self-fulfilling prophecy that, sadly, became true; her next 3 pregnancies would be miscarriages. It was heart-breaking to watch because she wanted a baby more than anything in the world. Every time I would see her or call to check on how she was doing in general, I knew it would be a response of depression. Sarah found it difficult to enjoy anything anymore whether it was a nice dinner, a great movie, and especially not baby showers or friends that came over to visit with their young children.

Finally her husband gave her some tough love. He told her that she needed to stop obsessing, let go, and try to enjoy her life. He said,

"If it's meant to be, then it will happen" and told her she needed to be patient. Maybe this seemed a bit insensitive but her thoughts and fears didn't allow for any other outcome than what kept happening. Sarah agreed to finally let go and leave it up to a higher power. She also learned to appreciate the time with her husband in her new marriage. Instead of focusing on sex just as an exercise to make a baby, they began bringing romance back into their relationship and enjoying some pleasure. For a couple that was married less than two years, this was crucial.

As they developed a stronger bond with each other and had more fun, Sarah started relaxing. Guess what happened? She became pregnant and they now have a beautiful one year old. Now that she knows she is capable of conceiving, the earlier fear has been removed and her body is no longer in a constant state of panic. If they decide to expand their family, it's likely this time around she'll be just fine.

* * *

If you live in a big city like New York, it's normal for men to not settle down until they're into their 40's and sometimes later. Half of my girlfriends have a fear of never getting married and becoming old maids. Statements like, "All men are jerks" or "Men just don't want to commit" have become declarations for many women as the absolute truth. To avoid being naïve following so many failed relationships with players, cheaters, and douche bags, it's almost understandable to take the stance that, "I expect you to hurt me like all the other guys."

Now the problem with this jaded expectation and belief system is that every guy they encounter will continue to show up as either a commitaphobe or just playing games. Even if you have been in 100 crappy relationships, this is a big world. Someone good is bound to appear if you are truly open. That also means you need to put yourself out there in ways that you never did before. Maybe you need to be willing to travel to another state or be set up on a blind date. When you do this, you're sending out an energetic message that you're open to meeting someone.

Being open is the opposite of being afraid. You may not have success through either one of these channels but - by shifting your consciousness - someone you walked past every day on the way to work may now turn around and say hi to you. A good guy who never saw you as a potential partner can suddenly view you in a new light. Prior to this, your subconscious message could only draw in the very guys you were scared of. Having negative expectations about relationships will only make the goal of marriage very delayed or unlikely.

If you catch yourself expecting the worst, talk yourself out of it and refocus. Make a list of all the things you want in a partner and how he should treat you. Be careful not to include the things you don't want; it's best not to bring any energy to those qualities. Watch and see what happens. The next guy you attract may not necessarily be your soul mate but he'll be different from all the ones before. Be patient! This process takes time. With a little practice you'll eventually call in the person that matches your desires rather than one who feeds into your fears.

* * *

If we haven't been hit personally by the unstable economy, all of us know people who have. With some friends, every conversation is always about not having money and how they're afraid things will never look up. If you're going through this, I would suggest changing your language. It's not that you can't be disappointed about the situation but you must have some conviction that things will get better.

Just meditating or thinking positive thoughts, however, are only part of the process. If you're not seeing any progress from a job that used to be fruitful, if your recruiter hasn't been helpful, or if there's nothing exciting in the "Sunday Times," try opening your mind to doing something else. Whether it's a total career change or switching to a related field, making a shift and getting your mind off of the problem can open up a window of success that you never imagined.

A few years ago I was let go from a project because the funding ran out. I loved what I was doing because it was in the health world, the hours were awesome, I got to travel, and the money was great. I thought this job was made for me and didn't want to now have to settle for something I wasn't passionate about while making half the salary.

Rather than get stuck waiting for my next dream opportunity to show up, I still kept my eyes open while also doing things that provided temporary income. Along the way, these temp jobs and side projects introduced me to people I would have otherwise never had access to. Even though the short term income didn't compare to what I was making before, the connections I made were priceless. I ended up getting several consulting offers through the new relationships I made and found an even better fit for me than the original project I was so upset about losing. I now have an amazing place to see clients that I would have needed to rent separately if this change didn't occur. Staying busy throughout that difficult period didn't allow time to focus on my fears. If I just sat home worrying how I'm going to pay my bills, I'd likely still be in the same position.

It's human nature to let our minds go to the worst possible scenario, especially if we've had a bad experience before. Remember that Fear is also lack of Faith. It takes practice but work on pushing away the fears and having faith that the right outcome will occur.

fifteen

Gotta Have Faith

Through all the disappointments, challenges, and not feeling "at home" with most situations or people, I don't think I'd be able to function if I didn't believe there was a divine reason for everything. My spirit would for sure be broken. Although we can't prove there's a higher power, I strongly believe that life is a series of lessons and that we were put in our unique bodies to have all the experiences we were given. People who walk around depressed all the time honestly can't believe this. If they did, they would know that suffering is a reflection of perspective and everything is about the way we cope. Just as children learn science, math, history, and the basic courses to make it through school, they should be taught principles of spirituality.

When my mother was told at age 35 she didn't have long to live, she was lucky to have her dear friend, Beverly, who gave her some faith. Beverly not only made a vow to look after me when she died, but also opened my mother's mind to her progressive beliefs about the soul, death, and reincarnation. She was gifted in her abilities to help remove the fear of death for friends and relatives that were passing.

To prepare for what was going to happen, Beverly encouraged my mother to study several books including *Many Lives Many Masters*, *Why Bad Things Happen to Good People*, and *Love, Medicine and Miracles*. Before she left this world, she truly believed that she had a mission to complete and it was over. I've never seen someone deal with the idea of death so convinced that this wasn't the end. I was left all of her reading materials and - for a 13 year old - the content was pretty heavy. The other kids in school were reading Judy Bloom novels.

I no longer had a mother, and my father was out of the picture. If there was such a thing as reincarnation, did it mean I chose my parents and my circumstances? Was I supposed to be alone with no brothers or sisters? Such were the questions that went into my thought process at that time. Strangely, I felt at peace in believing that my mother's soul was always with me. I'm familiar with the concept of having a guardian angel but I felt like it was my mother's own presence that stayed with me and kept me protected.

* * *

I began doing very deep soul-searching and all paths led to Eastern philosophy and healing modalities because I wanted to help people. My first teacher showed up when I was 18. His name was Lewis and he named his school "The Academy of Natural Healing."

Lewis wasn't at all what I expected. He was a Jewish guy from the Bronx and had been doing spiritual studies for over 20 years. He learned from Shamans and far-out healers and would share his teachings with a lot of charisma and personality. Often his mannerisms would make me laugh and his joking around could be borderline inappropriate if you didn't have a sense of humor. His classes were totally unorthodox but I was only 18 and had nothing else to compare it to. It was pretty normal for us to be giving each other reflexology in the middle of a lecture or do some kind of Reiki healing. During our breaks, I'd run to the health food store on West 72nd street and grab a green juice and a side of brown rice. My whole lifestyle changed. I was living in the East Village, started eating only vegan, and my personal look was either hipster or bohemian depending on the season.

I really got into yoga during this period and went regularly to the shala in Soho to study with Eddie Stern. Eddie was another teacher that I assumed had Jewish roots, too, but I never actually asked him. I was often entertained by his clever wit while being contorted in a painful posture. Sometimes I wanted to laugh and cry at the same time. Although, through his close relationship with

Patthabi Jois - the original guru of Ashtanga Yoga – he was nothing short of authentic. I learned from these two examples of how the real spiritual teachers never took themselves too seriously. It was the fakers that put on the air of only seriousness and being holier than thou. He never even advertised and it was almost impossible to get a space to practice and squeeze in your mat unless you showed up really early.

I started practicing daily at 6 a.m. - even on Sundays! My apartment took on the yoga theme and began looking like an ashram. I hung huge posters of Shiva and Ganesha, the Hindu Deities, on my wall. I laugh now because I thought I was so enlightened back then. I believed I had a better understanding of the world than other people because – unlike most of them - I knew some sacred teachings.

Yet even with all the yoga, meditating and spiritual work I did, I felt something was missing. The more I immersed myself in that world, the lonelier I became. All these rituals and teachings I had been learning that were derived from Asia, India, and the Far East were concepts I certainly respected but it didn't feel like my tribe.

* * *

Although I was Jewish, I never knew anything about my own faith. My mother remarried someone who was Catholic. My father was removed and also an atheist. I never had a Bat Mitzvah or really spent time in a synagogue growing up. My limited perception of Judaism was just a lot of strict rules that made no sense. I was still proud, however, to be a Jew because my grandparents were Holocaust survivors. I was also intrigued by great Jewish minds such as Albert Einstein and some of my favorite comedians - Jackie Mason and Mel Brooks.

I ended up attending a lecture with a Rebbetzin named Esther Jungreis on the Upper East Side. This woman was very petite in stature but she was a pillar of strength. Esther was a Holocaust survivor, a widow, a wonderful mother, and a grandmother. Her lessons would be about the "Parsha" which meant the Torah portion of the week. I knew nothing about the Bible but she somehow made it relevant to what was currently going on in the world.

She would also infuse mysticism, numerology, and connect the past to the present. I would listen to the biblical stories of all these great matriarchs and patriarchs and their challenges. Whether any of these things really happened is up to interpretation, but I found myself identifying with these characters. The greatest people in history didn't grow up with a silver spoon; instead, they dealt with horrible tragedies, betrayal, jealousy, abandonment, and every painful emotion I had ever experienced times1000. Instead of being victims, they rose above their circumstance and became examples for mankind to emulate.

For me, this all lead to the question of why do some people have it so easy and others are constantly tested with challenges. Does God love people more who have happier, easier lives? I had never really believed that was the case, but Esther was sure to point out that we are actually closest to God when we trust in faith and ask for help.

No one calls out for help when everything is awesome, she explained, but only when everything is a mess, when we're feeling hopeless, and when we can't see the light on the other side. To my surprise I also learned that Judaism acknowledged ideas of reincarnation, and that dietary kosher laws weren't just for health but for spiritual reasons, too. It was amazing to see the similarities between Judaism and Eastern religions. This was not typically spoken about in mainstream Jewish circles with the exception of what they teach at The Kabbalah Center.

Unfortunately, the more I immersed myself in organized religion, the more I witnessed closed-mindedness, judgment and hypocrisy. So many "religious" people I encountered weren't necessarily spiritual or even good people. They did things because they grew up that way or maybe because they wanted to fit into a community.

I came to realize that there are beautiful lessons in every religion and spiritual practice, but you can apply those principles that personally resonate with you. You don't have to take a stance on just one and dismiss all the others.

Whether you connect to God through prayer, chanting or meditation, it doesn't matter as long as it feels good to you. I sometimes will sit in my room before bed and have a heart-to-heart conversation with God asking for help, guidance, and clarity. I will also set an intention for what I want to manifest and put it out in the universe. It's kind of scary but I tend to see things unfold pretty quickly. Everything I have ever seriously focused on or prayed for has actually happened. Maybe it's not in the exact way I wished for but I'd always receive some sideways version of my request.

Our thoughts are powerful and we need to be careful about what we ask for and put out energetically. This also shows us that - with some faith and conviction - we all have the ability to change our circumstance for the better.

sixteen

Use Your Powers for the Good

All of us have God-given gifts. Whether it's intelligence, creativity, great communication skills, artistic abilities, natural beauty, or incredible wealth, never lose sight of the reality that you can lose it. While it's easy to become arrogant when you're constantly being reminded of how wonderful you are, look at how many times celebrities who become the "It" guy or girl are quickly forgotten the following year.

On a smaller scale, even our own achievements can still go to our heads. Usually the more ego we have when displaying them, the more likely we'll have to be taught a lesson. Karma has a funny way of showing up at inconvenient times. Whether you were simply blessed or worked your ass off for your success, consider yourself lucky and not entitled. When you expect that these gifts are always coming to you, don't be surprised in the near future to receive a rude awakening!

Throughout my life, losses have been all too familiar. There were plenty of times when everything seemed to be working out perfectly – the man in my life was solid, business opportunities were coming easily, and my social life with friends was exciting. Suddenly – and without any warning whatsoever – everything took an ugly turn.

Young people, I think, are especially susceptible to being caught off-guard. They can't – and don't – anticipate any curve balls being thrown at them because they mistakenly assume that challenges won't arise until later in life. When conflicts with my health or problems with business associates showed up unexpectedly, they literally turned my world upside down in ways similar to what I experienced growing up. While my friends were focused on parties, dating, and hip social events, I was trying to push out the thought of, "Oh my God, I don't want to be sick forever and not able to afford the roof over my head."

Without health and financial means, it's really hard to function and pretend that everything is fine. Still, I had no choice but to deal with what was happening and know that through my past circumstances I always turned out okay. I simply refused to accept any other outcome! Just as I believed I would, I did get healthier and was able to rebuild my business – an outcome that left me with a much different mindset that I am now so grateful for.

You see, I had always assumed that I was karmically squared up with God because of my rough childhood. I didn't get why new problems were arising and thought (but not in a mean way) it was only fair that the next person who had an easier path should get hit, not me. Unfortunately, going through a few really bad things doesn't necessarily spare you later on. Although, disaster certainly can bypass you down the road, it's only if you learned the lesson and changed as a result of your hardship.

When I was at my worst physically and financially, I spent time reflecting and thinking about what I had truly learned from my past. I even thought at one point that my life was on the line. If I was to die, what would people say about me? Maybe they would say that I was dynamic, smart, spiritual, possibly sweet (but only if we were close – I've been told I have an aloof vibe), and probably pretty. That doesn't sound like a bad list, but what was missing was a "loving partner or a great friend."

I had done a lot of work on myself for myself but not necessarily sharing what I had learned with others. I, therefore, came to the conclusion that my nature had always been somewhat selfish. I prayed and tried to make deals with God to give me another chance and the opportunity to change if it would take me out of my circumstance. I looked back at my life from the beginning as if I were Ebenezer Scrooge being visited by the ghosts in *A Christmas Carol*. I replayed all of my past romantic relationships, friendships, and even interactions with strangers. I became aware of so many of my mistakes and how I may have hurt others even if it was unintentional.

I always had a good heart but could have dealt with people much better – especially boyfriends. Although communication is one of my greatest strengths, I realized that I always ran away from situations whenever things didn't work out. Sometimes this would leave men feeling totally confused, hurt, and even abandoned – none of which was ever my intention.

What I was supposed to gain from my challenges was compassion, but instead I shut down and was devoid of feelings with anyone who tried to get close to me. When people – especially men – showed too much emotion over anything, I couldn't deal with it and flawed them for being weak. Here I was now ALONE. I'm sure any one of those guys would have stuck it out with me through my rough patch. Instead, there was no one around to listen whenever I approached a point where I wanted to cry and be weak.

This experience taught me that you can never stop working on yourself despite how much crap you may have endured. Again, I had a bit of an ego believing that since I survived such a big storm early on, I should automatically get a hall pass. Perhaps I even felt entitled that a good guy, success, and health were obviously going to just be there no matter what because I deserved these things. When everything at one point starting coming to me easily, I actually stopped thinking about how hard I once had it.

A lot of people don't stop to feel grateful when things are good. When you're sitting in the power seat, though, it's really only a privilege. I often wonder if that's why I had to experience so many difficult relationships later on. Sometimes karma can take a lifetime to come full circle, but starting in my late 20's it was like the rounds of karmic ammunition were just shooting at me. I had to always question, "How did I get here and what do I need to do to lessen this decree of all the chaos in my life?"

Going through triumph can be very sobering. Life can be wonderful but how easily we forget to work on ourselves when we're feeling like, "This is as great as it gets!" Through having experienced pain in so many areas, I more often root for the underdog and am ultra-sensitive listening to conversations where people make fun of others for what they lack. Even if you're guilty of being critical of others, it doesn't mean you're a bad person. It just may be a reflection of always having things go your way. The cool, popular kids at school wouldn't just ask the nerds to come sit with them at lunch unless maybe they had a little brother or sister that was bullied and they somehow related to them through a past personal experience.

You'd think that we'd grow up at some point but these behaviors don't necessarily develop on their own with age. When you have gifts and people call upon you to share with them, you need to remember that this isn't happening by accident. In the past, I used to be annoyed when people wanted things from me. My feeling was, "I did it on my own and so can you." But being strong and independent was actually one of my gifts. I clearly understand now that overcoming challenges should be a stepping stone and a way to help people not to take the same turns. It's not to gloat and tell yourself how wonderful you are. (And by the way, no one ever has an easy journey!) One of the lessons I learned was how to be vulnerable and share the mistakes I made along the way. Being vulnerable is one of the best ways to help others feel understood.

I've never met a successful person that didn't screw up. Unfortunately, the ego often takes over when they get to the top and they forget the small people. Whether it's the ugly duckling that turned into the swan, the fat kid who became a hot shot personal trainer, or the geek who now runs his own hedge fund, it's important to stay grounded and remember what brought you to this place and the people that helped to mold you.

You don't have to wait for a crisis to occur to reflect on how you could be a better person. It feels like God had to light a fire up my ass to help me grow. I'm strangely thankful for my falls but if there was a better way to get the lesson sans the drama, I would have taken it. Be honest with yourself and think about whether you're spoiled from your blessings or if you recognize them as gifts. Whether we use our wealth to be philanthropic, use our communication to teach, or our wisdom to heal others, share these gifts with the world. That's the best way to hold onto them.

seventeen

Do What You Love

One thing I decided at a very young age was that I couldn't accept being mediocre. I always had big dreams of making my mark in this world, helping humanity, and being a success - whatever that meant. It's not unusual for children to have grand aspirations but, as reality sets in, there are also self-imposed limitations that come with being an adult. It's normal for a lot of individuals to resist change and avoid risks because of their fears of the unknown. Accordingly, they often take the safe route like the rest of their friends and family members.

As young adults, most people are taught that they need to get a good education, make an honest living that pays the bills, find someone to marry, and pop out a couple of kids. That message, however, was never impressed upon me, much less pounded into my head on a daily basis. Because I was on my own at very young age and didn't have parents constantly whispering into my ears, I lived mostly on instinct and survival. To me, life always had the appearance of being pretty short. It made me never want to complete my journey as a boring one with regret if I died tomorrow.

Even though I believe in reincarnation and that this is not our only life, I wouldn't want to waste this life as Danielle Pashko on just being like everyone else. I've taken a lot of criticism for not doing things an easier way. It's not that I'm rebellious or a nonconformist; I just do things in general from a very right brain perspective. I operate from my gut in all matters. Whether it's professional, relationships, or important life decisions, I can't let something happen if I don't feel at peace in my heart.

* * *

After having very little of a relationship with my father, I asked to move in with him and his new wife after my mother died. Since they both worked in sales, they had to travel a lot and just weren't around all that much. There were occasions, for instance, they'd be on business trips to different parts of the country at the same time. This meant that they'd leave me in the apartment alone for sometimes up to five days. That's kind of crazy for a freshman in high school but keep in mind that I was super mature for my age.

On the one hand I thought it was really cool to have so much freedom. The downside is that they didn't leave me any money for groceries and I didn't have transportation to get to class. I was left walking pretty far in the mornings and had my girlfriend, Claudia, sleep over all the time so I wouldn't be alone at night. She'd tell her parents that we were doing homework and come bearing tons of food; her parents were Italian and amazing cooks. The two of us were young girls but dressed up like we were 25. The tight jeans, high heels, and heavy eye makeup were part of our look. We were dressed for a night club just to go to school or a stroll in the mall. When I was home, I'd sit glued to MTV, completely obsessed with my hero, Madonna. I was so intrigued by her because not only was she sexy and fabulous but she was also a visionary that reinvented herself over and over again. Like me, her own mother had died at a young age and she left home to move to the big city and pursue her dreams.

I thought, "I have dreams, too, and they are not to be sitting around in Florida. I want to go to New York."

Remarkably, I manifested this ambition in a matter of weeks.

As it turned out, my stepmother returned home from a business trip ahead of my father. We were sitting together in the kitchen when she announced, "My children are already grown and your father is never around. It's not my responsibility to raise any more kids. This is really not working out."

I had only been living with them for a few months and I'm already getting kicked out? My father wasn't even in the conversation but when he was later informed of her decision, he never bothered to interject. So now I had to find where to go.

I began looking through my address book to determine which friends had parents cool enough to let me stay with them. Then it dawned on me: I have an aunt and uncle in New York! I knew that with two kids in only a one bedroom apartment they barely had space for a fifth person. The older boy who was already 6'2" lived in the back of the rail road style kitchen. His legs were long enough to still brush up against the refrigerator and the daughter slept in what looked like a bunk bed in the living room. She slept on the top bunk and the lower part was used for storage. This meant that I would get the couch but I was still committed to making this happen. I called them up and did the best to charm them and pull on their sympathy strings. They agreed and I packed up my bags and left.

I was thrilled! I should have been feeling a little upset that my dad basically dumped me after my mother just passed earlier in the year, but I felt like this was an opportunity to reinvent my life and start all over again. I was too young at that time to have a clear picture of exactly what I wanted to do, but I knew that living in New York was a promising start that could lead me in a positive direction.

* * *

Like most high school students who study hard for standardized tests and have at least some clue what they want to pursue in college, I did things a little backwards. I wanted to find out "who I was" before I committed myself to a job that defined me.

Looking back, I know very few people that have explored more professions than I did. Starting at 17 years old I worked in the night clubs bartending or as a door girl while I was pursuing modeling. I then went to school to become a licensed massage therapist, a certified yoga instructor, and a nutritional consultant. In between I explored other interests that were kind of out-of-the-box. My craziest experience was working with professional Sumo wrestlers for a world championship.

I also dabbled in image consulting, blogging on dating websites, and consulting for anti-aging doctors. You name it, I wanted to try it - and this was all by the age of 30. It may sound a little crazy, but I'm happy I got it out of my system early. I won't be having a mid-life crisis or regretting that I hadn't done something more exciting or fulfilling.

Even though it may appear I'm a Jill of all Trades, having those experiences helped me to be laser-focused professionally. Once you are clear on what you don't want, you can pursue exactly what you do want without interruption or temptation. There's something to be said for enjoying what you do and actually getting paid well to do it. As a result, I love my weekdays as much as the weekends.

Truth be told, I've known no shortage of people who make a lot of money in very respectable professions but the most exciting part of their day is their lunch break. These are the same people – and maybe you're even one of them – who spend the entire year looking forward to their four-week vacation. They know they're not happy but that "safe" harbor of a steady paycheck has crushed their spirit to ever imagine anything different. While I'd never say, "So why don't you just quit?" I think it's essential to have a side business or creative outlet that makes the hard work and lack of fulfillment at least worth it.

Some people may define you by your career, I believe success is more accurately measured in how happy you are. The whole purpose of making a lot of money is to afford all the luxuries that bring plea-sure. Once we acquire those things, however - the designer bag, the shoes, and the new dress - the good feeling we experience is only fleet-ing. I appreciate nice things and don't think it's superficial at all to strive for them, but passion for life and waking up with a mission every day is something that is long-lasting.

Whatever your given talent is, don't be afraid to share it. It's no accident that you have a specific gift. Let's say you've always wanted to pursue acting. What's the big deal if you move to LA for a year and start making the rounds of auditions? If you live in Milwaukee and always dreamed of being a fashion designer, why not check out Paris or New York? If you're underpaid but the top earner at your position, maybe you should consider starting a new business on your own. Is there a book in your head you've always wanted to write? If you diligently committed to only one page a day for a full year, you'd have 365 pages to show for it. (The average-length novel, by the way, is 320.)

If you feel stuck, take some time to think about what inspires you and if it's realistic. Ask people you trust to tell you what talents and skill sets come to mind when they think about what you're really good at. Identify what kind of training, mentoring and resources you'll need in order to bring your dreams into the realm of possibility. If you're single and don't have children yet, this should be the most experimental time in your life.

The world is yours to take on. As you create the story of your life, make it a good one!

eighteen

Ready For The Moment

Whatever the dream you've had your heart set on, you've probably spent a lot of time wondering when "The Moment" will arrive that will actually make your dream come true. The question is, though, how many moments have already slipped past because you didn't recognize them for what they really were; specifically, invitations to say "yes" and take a bold leap of faith?

Consider, for instance, the person who wants to be discovered for her singing abilities. She goes to the concert of one of her favorite performers and imagines what it would be like to be up there onstage. In an unexpected twist, the performer suddenly says, "Hey, I'd like to do a duet. Anybody here know the words to such and such?" The aspiring singer can't believe her ears. She knows the lyrics to such-and-such by heart but is reluctant to raise her hand and volunteer. Why? Because she's wearing the wrong outfit that evening or her hair isn't perfect or any number of other excuses she can think of to justify that this just isn't the way she always pictured her big moment would be. While she's busy agonizing about this, the performer is already handing the microphone to someone else, someone who recognizes a golden opportunity when she sees one.

All right, it's not a given that such an act of spontaneity would have yielded a fabulous recording contract but she'll never know, will she? By the time she realizes what has just been offered, that train will have left the station…and might not make a return trip.

* * *

My teacher Lewis Harrison's mantra was, "Always say 'yes' unless the cost is too high."

I first heard this phrase when I was 18 and tried to figure out how I might apply it to my life at that particular time. While I was too young to offer much of my own knowledge or wisdom to others, I had access to a lot of well connected people and self-starter types who were intrigued by my unconventional upbringing and wanted to take me under their wing. Socializing with people my parents' age taught me a great deal about business, how to be an entrepreneur, and how to use appropriate language to earn respect. I never wanted to be misleading by accepting invitations to lunch or dinner – especially those offered by the opposite sex – but I also knew that cultivating relationships with successful business people could lead to opportunities and connections down the road. Thus, I would never be too flirtatious and yet contributed enough to each interaction to make it appealing enough for those very busy power house executives to want to be in my company. I learned that as long as I was clear and upfront about my agenda, it wasn't my problem if someone else wanted more.

With the passage of each year, a wider range of opportunities presented themselves to me. "Yes" became the most frequently used word in my vocabulary. By learning to be an awesome networker, I discovered I could collect lots of new acquaintances at social events. Those people would then invite me to other functions and I never wanted to turn down a chance to meet their contacts. Accordingly, I am probably one of the few people that never used a resume to get a job.

To clarify, I wasn't networking to make "friends"; I was networking to create prospects that would open doors. I was clear that I wanted these interactions to translate into dollars. Until I had a better idea about what my professional goals were, I just wanted opportunities in the health and beauty business and so I put myself into situations to meet the people who could help me. Who knew that I'd be offered so many kinds of jobs that were out of the scope of what I knew how to do!

When I was 24 I was running a mobile spa company that offered yoga, massage, and facials; this was basically all I was ever trained for. At the time I was hired to help organize a spa event for All Star Weekend in Los Angeles, I thought it would be cool to have some healthy products to give away. Through my social network, I knew some people at a nutritional company that produced vitamins and supplements. I pitched them to give me lots of free products for gift bags and they were so impressed with how I sold them that they subsequently offered me a consulting job.

They next asked if I could call on doctors that were selling their products in the same way I had presented to them. Well, I knew nothing about sales but the compensation was great and I could still run my business on the side. I said "yes" and let them train me. It wasn't just about the money but more about the access. I knew I wanted to launch my own product line independently or with a doctor at one point, and this could be a great chance to meet all the top dermatologists, plastic surgeons, and medical specialists in the city.

When I started working on this new path, I had no idea what I was doing. I hadn't mastered the art of getting appointments over the phone and unless I got in front of my target, the deal would never happen. My 30-second elevator pitch really sucked. I knew that if I just got to meet these doctors in person, I could sell them anything. So I had to get a little creative and work with whatever I could use. I came up with the idea of adding a photo to my email signature like some of the real estate agents do. Maybe it wasn't as professional as, let's say, a thorough explanation on a recently published review from The Cleveland Clinic, but a winning smile goes a long way…

Not only did I learn quickly on my feet but I also studied heavily. This enabled me to become as knowledgeable as my counterparts to the degree that I was able to custom formulate products for doctors who wanted to create their own product lines. Some of the most intelligent physicians hired and relied on me for my understanding of nutraceuticals.

After just one year of doing this, I accomplished exactly what I had hoped for. I built relationships with all of the top doctors and many of them even asked me to be a part of their team. Whether it was helping them open a medi-spa, develop a product line, build their website, handle marketing or do public relations, I figured it out. Keep in mind that many of these skills for a start-up company required someone with a strong head for business. Despite the reality that I never went to business school - my education was in holistic health and nutrition - I always accepted these propositions as if I were fully qualified and capable.

Here's how my strategy worked. Before I began any of these new assignments, I'd park myself at Barnes and Noble and read every book I could find on whatever particular skill set I was asked to perform (within reason of course). As far as anyone knew when I came in to start, I was an expert. Some may call it bullshitting, but I prefer to call it hustling. Having the attitude of "I can take on whatever life throws at me" will leave you with boundless opportunity. Every day you are open to possibilities, something will show up. Yes, there are obviously professions such as being a surgeon, lawyer, or engineer where you can't just wing it without formal training but there are certainly plenty of moments in life where your talent gets discovered if you just say "yes."

Look at it this way: If something is offered to you, it usually means that someone sees your potential. I like to remind myself that if I try it and don't like it or I don't seem to be succeeding, I can always politely withdraw and go do something else. Most people, however, are so scared to fail that they would rather lose an opportunity than look stupid. My response is, "How do you know unless you at least try?"

There have been several times that I have been asked to give a presentation or accept an interview on a topic I knew fairly well but perhaps was not quite an expert. You can't tell an editor or a producer of an event or TV show, "Can I think about it and get back to you?" If you flinch, there are 100 other people just dying to take your spot. Rather than miss the boat, I always accept the challenge and make sure to prepare myself within the timeframe allotted, even if it means cancelling whatever other engagements I have and using that time to read non-stop until the scheduled appearance.

The first time you're asked to do something on a big scale, it will always be intimidating. Even the understudy who has rehearsed daily for a Broadway performance will feel scared at the moment when the star unexpectedly gets sick and they have to shine.

These special moments are not coincidences. The truth is that we've been thinking/dreaming/fantasizing about them for as long as we can remember and eventually they just manifest into fruition. If you don't take action when that window of opportunity opens, you may not get a second chance. And if you do go for it, it doesn't really matter if you're not successful the first time around; you'll get a second chance before you know it. That's just the way things work. Falling on your face is only a reminder that you're human. Learn to laugh at yourself. Each time you pick yourself back up, you chip away a little more at the fear. The scariest thing in the world becomes second nature and eventually you'll be excelling at things you never imagined with confidence and ease.

Learn to get excited for these moments. We create our own destiny and the key is to say "yes" to one opportunity at a time.

nineteen

You're Stronger than You Think

Why do some people have all the luck and you have it so hard? I guess it all depends on what you consider to be "lucky."

No one has everything and we're all constantly tested with challenges - some much more difficult than others. It's hard to perceive coping with things that are extremely difficult until we are actually faced with them. Just because the pain of a situation may bring on fear, anxiety, depression or uncertainty, it doesn't mean that you're weak. What's important is to acknowledge those uncomfortable feelings rather than dismissing them and denying their existence. Nor should you have to feel ashamed that your situation seems insignificant compared to people who are starving in Africa or your grandparents who are Holocaust survivors. Everything is relative to what is familiar to you. Once you sit for a while with that pain from your disappointment, you then need to learn to tap into your own unique strengths that can pull you out. While some of these strengths are more obvious, others must be uncovered.

As I have shared throughout this book, my childhood and teenage years were full of pain. Losing my mother, having an abusive stepfather, an absent biological father, not fitting in after going to four different high schools, exposure to drugs all around, and having to support myself at 16 when I was basically poor – no, this was not a charmed life by any stretch of the imagination! If I was another child and you told me that all of these things were going to happen, I'd say, "There's no way I can possibly handle it."

It's amazing, though, how we're wired to tap into survival mode when we need to. It's like the story of the mother who lifted up a car to rescue her baby. The fight or flight response kicks in and we do what we need to do if our life or the life of someone we love is at stake. Throughout my adolescence and into young adulthood I had to think fast on my feet and say, "Okay, how can I get out of this situation and have some stability going forward? How can I make a living with no one helping me?" I wasn't a great student. I was a terrible test-taker and scored horribly on my S.A.T.'s. I also knew the schools that would accept me weren't the top-tier universities. I remember thinking, "I'm never going to be a doctor, lawyer, or high powered businesswoman. I need to find a way to hustle."

What I did have going for me was that even though I wasn't "book smart" per se, I had more emotional intelligence than anyone else my age - and years beyond - because of all my hardships. I was a good communicator, very presentable, and always articulate. I absorbed much more in the school of life than in a classroom. Given the opportunity to meet them in person, people always liked me. It, therefore, became clear that doing something related to building relationships would become my greatest strength. Instead of dwelling on all of the things I felt I was lacking, I embraced my ability to read people and to be sensitive to their personal and/or health related struggles. Little did I know at the time that the groundwork was being laid for my becoming a wellness consultant.

It's interesting to witness how the scales are always balanced. You could be fabulously rich and yet somehow feel lonely and unfulfilled. You may have so much love and a wonderful family but money may not come easy to you. You might have everything going for you but get sick or lose a loved one. You could even be drop-dead gorgeous but find that you're the last single one out of all your friends who are now happily married. It's a lesson to not be jealous - because no one has everything.

* * *

Even when I felt like I was doing a good job of coping with my past-experiencing divorce, followed by a string of crappy relationships, getting cancer and going broke made me feel like the ground under me was so unstable that I could sink at any minute. After hitting rock bottom, the revelation I had was that I had to change my thinking.

I literally began to look at every challenge as a pass/fail test. Each time something really bad happened, it became a game to me. Now let me make clear that I definitely slipped - that's part of being human - but quickly I had to work on removing myself from the situation as if I were observing as an outsider. I wouldn't allow myself to fall into a depression. Sometimes I'd try to become a problem-solver but other times I had to give up my fears and have some faith. We all know the expression, "We plan and God laughs." It's easy to think an aspect of strength is to always be in control, but strength actually comes from allowing the right outcome to occur. I began to realize that when things didn't go my way - when the relationship didn't work out, when the job that seemed like a dream was lost - it was all part of a bigger picture leading me to where I needed to be. There were so many times that these so called catastrophes even saved my life.

None of that was apparent, of course, while I was actually enduring the experience. Only when the reasons for the hardship were revealed to me much later did I finally learn I could take each situation and understand why it had to go down exactly the way it did. Although things seemed bad, the pain was only temporary and I was always okay in the end. I just had a choice whether to suffer or ride the situation and expect to move through it. When you stop to think about it, it's not much different than rough air or turbulence on a plane.

For many people, it's a lot easier to assume a victim mentality. That approach, however, typically leads them down a road of unhappiness, potential substance abuse, and always placing blame on others. When I was told I had thyroid cancer, for instance, I thought, "More shit? Really?" As much as I had been terrified of this moment ever manifesting, I strangely felt a sense of calm when it actually hit. I had two choices: I could feel defeated or I could use all the tools that I had been armed with from all my studying. After all, I was a yoga teacher, I counseled clients nutritionally, and I had tremendous faith in God. Was I going to suddenly be a little mouse and forget everything I based my existence on?!

I decided I was going to handle this like a champion. Not that I'm at all in the same category, but how would Buddha, Jesus or Moses face this situation? When I was at the hospital the day of my surgery, I remember joking around with my anesthesiologist and the surgeon before I went under. I also forced myself to smile and visualize coming out healthy when the procedure was over. Although I was wobbly and not feeling so hot when I woke up, I kept my mind strong. From then on after, that's what I did.

Whether you feel weak physically or emotionally, a strong mind is what will give you the drive to get through your challenge. When I had crappy days, I refused to give energy to my weakness. It didn't stop me from gently exercising, doing restorative yoga, or anything physical that gave my body confidence. I had to work my way back up to where I used to be but it all started with small steps. At this moment I'm totally better and my body is stronger than ever. In many ways, I feel like it was a blessing. I don't take things for granted, and it was a great lesson on how to look fear in the face and work through it.

* * *

Some of our greatest accomplishments are during the scariest times. In many ways it's like training to prepare you for the next challenge. Whether you're a parent, spouse, business owner, or in a position that you are relied upon by others, having experienced tough challenges will help you to stay composed and reinforce a sense of calm and stability to everyone around you. There's always one person that is the glue holding the whole family or the business together. Is that person you?

Train yourself not to fall apart. Instead of watching too much Reality TV, rent a martial arts movie (or one of my favorites such as *Rocky* on Netflix) and tap into your inner warrior. Life has great moments but it's definitely a series of ups and downs. If everything is easy and you don't have challenges, there's not much incentive to grow and become a better person. Without pain, we are blind to blessings.

The next time you think you can't get through your dilemma, remove yourself from your situation for a minute. Try to be objective as an observer and give yourself the advice you'd dispense if you were mentoring a good friend. Have trust that your circumstance is only temporary and you will move through this. It's your choice to handle it with pain or be at peace with the outcome, even if it's not the one you want.

When you handle things in a high light - meaning from a place of faith and conviction - you will see later why everything had to unfold the way it did. Remember we all have the ability to cope within us. We are never faced with challenges we cannot handle.

twenty

We Write the Script

What if you were handed a magic pen and told that whatever you wrote down would later come to fruition? Could you be clear in your intentions and articulate everything you dreamed for down to the most descriptive details? It's likely you may consider yourself too intelligent to believe something like that could ever possibly work - but that's the mistake most of us make. When I talk about writing, the exercise doesn't necessarily have to be done in that way. We can also call in our most desired outcomes by practicing visualization and imagining ourselves in the very place that we want to be.

If you've seen the movie *The Secret*, it's probably not the first time you've heard about this Law of Attraction stuff. I first learned about these practices from my mother when I was 12 years old. When she was going through her cancer treatments, she would meditate on a daily basis and visualize seeing herself healthy. She would close her eyes, scan her body, and imagine that everything was fully healed and operating perfectly. She would then say positive affirmations and use the power of language to make her feel better. She also used homeopathic remedies and did things that were considered unconventional for the medical community. Although the cancer had already spread too far to revert back, she amazed the doctors by surpassing the few months of life she was originally told she would live and lasted for five more years.

From that point in my life I, too, began performing visualizations and writing down my aspirations. Although I saw a few small miracles, I wasn't sure if it was really working until just recently. It literally took 20 years to manifest but it's all happening. I think the delay in everything coming together fully was because I couldn't clearly visualize the exact life I wanted. I was only seeing half of the picture. When someone asked me, "What do you want to do with your life," I would say something along the lines of, "I want to be like Marianne Williamson or Louise Hay who were both famous authors who wrote books on health, spirituality, and healing. I also want to speak on these issues."

What did that really mean, though? Oftentimes we can't even grasp having something until we are in circumstances that can realistically put us there. At 18 or 19 years old when I had these career goals, I wasn't clear at all on how I was going to achieve them. People would say, "Well, that's cute or nice or whatever, but how do you expect to make any money?" That was a good question. The things that I wanted to do seemed much too esoteric for people to grasp so I had to pursue other related job skills while still keeping my end goal in mind.

As the years passed, I kept being drawn to professions that ultimately would lead me to that very place I wanted to end up. When I was doing things such as being a massage therapist, yoga instructor, or nutritionist, I wasn't sure how any of that would translate to writing or speaking or helping the masses but it did, in fact, show up. Consider how our world is rapidly changing through social media and, thus, making it easier than ever to connect with people we once never had access to. Anything you want to manifest is really at your fingertips. Who could have imagined even 10 years ago that you could have a thought and one second later you could type a few keys and thousands of people could hear your message!

But wait, I'm getting ahead of myself…

Although things seemed to be moving in the right direction, my visualizations weren't fine tuned enough. Unless you have a tremendous amount of inner stillness, it's extremely difficult to visualize without distractions or keep negative thoughts from spoiling your creation. Self- doubt likes to talk us out of our focus a lot of the time, so I think writing can sometimes be more effective - or needs to at least be done in conjunction with meditation. Even if we don't necessarily believe the things we want can happen, we can still put those dreams into words instead of just letting them float around aimlessly in the ether. It's easier, for instance, to describe your perfect man on a piece of paper than see him in your mind. The same goes for your dream job or dream lifestyle.

The catch?

Don't become so fixated on specific conditions and attributes that you end up giving yourself absolutely no room for flexibility – i.e., "My dream guy has to be David Beckham's twin brother!" What if you say that you can only imagine yourself working for the XYZ law firm or a particular fashion house? How do you know that your unique talents wouldn't have been better suited somewhere else…and at a much higher salary? How do you know that the employer you had your heart so fervently set on won't go bankrupt in two years or be embroiled in scandal? And how many girls did you know back in high school whose highest and best dream was to marry the campus jock…without considering he could turn into an unemployed couch potato with a beer belly and a wandering eye?

No matter who or what you believe in as an entity with the power to hear prayers and grant wishes, you have to approach the process with two understandings:

The first is that whatever you say might be taken literally and could be subject to celestial interpretation.

The second is that you can't expect your desires to manifest if you never take the time to actually define them.

This is where writing things down can create shifts for you. I believe I want children, for instance, but since I'm not married, it's hard for me to imagine myself pregnant or playing with my own kids. Still, it's not difficult for me to state this desire as long as I add the caveat "when the time is right and I can provide a good life for them."

What I believe I have control over can go something like this:

Relationship - My soul mate is ready for me and we are a perfect match. He is kind, spiritual, mature, tall, attractive, athletic, silly at times, and very successful. He loves me unconditionally and will be by my side through the good and bad. He appreciates my struggles, does not judge me, and I can feel comfortable to be myself around him. He only has eyes for me, does not play games, and knows he wants to spend his life with me. He is not impressed by the superficial because he is already confident in himself. We have incredible intimacy and can't wait to build a beautiful family together. We bring out each other's best qualities, challenge one another (in a good way!), and as a team we become better individuals. He protects me and with him I feel safe and at home.

Career - I have a thriving Wellness practice. Through teaching clients healthy lifestyle, diet, exercise habits, and faith, I am helping to create positive shifts in their lives. My clientele is primarily in New York, but I have satellite offices in Miami and Los Angeles. Additionally, I use Skype to counsel clients throughout the world. My books are bestsellers and the people who read them not only find that they relate to my struggles but that my advice inspires them to live more healthy, meaningful lives. Speaking publicly is easy for me because my message is sincere. I will make my first million dollars by 2015 and have enough money to share with friends and loved ones that are struggling.

You'll notice in these examples that I didn't say "My dream guy has dark hair, brown eyes and is 6 foot 3 inches" or "I am seeing 50 clients a week professionally." I purposely didn't address those levels of specificity because even though I'd be happy to have these dreams come true, I'm also comfortable with knowing that the right outcome will reveal itself. The best suited man for me could be blonde or I may do better professionally with fewer clients because writing will have become more of a priority. We can want things - but it's better not to be rigid. Set forth your desires, yet be open to the way they show up. We can't possibly know what's best for us on all occasions - that's just part of being human. What's more important is to know your mission. Then let God or the universe do their work to make it happen in a way that will be for your highest good.

* * *

While writing and visualizing, we must be conscious of our actions. We need to put ourselves in the right environment and make deliberate choices to have our story play out the way we want.

If, for instance, you're committed to losing 20 pounds, you need to do more than meditate on being thin and speaking to your nutritionist about it; you need to actually go to the store to buy healthy food, eat fewer calories, and exercise more. The same goes for having more money. If you are commission-based and your well has dried up, start going to networking events, take a social media class so people can find you online, or figure out a creative way to drum up more business.

I know this information sounds redundant, but we can either continue to be stuck in a place of complaints or take action and change our fate. While talk therapy has merit, it's not always helpful to keep regurgitating the same things we already know and yet still do nothing. It's very nice that someone can tell me that I'm validated in feeling upset, anxious, depressed, or whatever - but how will that honestly improve things if I don't move on to the next chapter?

Nothing is permanent. Whatever we want to achieve (within reason) is really in our hands. The first step is to trust that it's actually possible and move forward. Our past wasn't meant to defeat us but all too frequently it messes with us to the point we become crippled. The result of continuously being beaten down is that we become prevented from accomplishing what our soul came into this world to do.

As a child, things happen to us that we're not trained to handle. As adults, though, we're capable of real maturity; specifically, the spiritual kind. Tell yourself that grown-ups don't hold grudges, feel victimized, or feel unworthy. That's the whole test of life. This is one of the hardest things to do, but in reality no one has actual power over you. We are the only real opponents.

Your book of life can be wonderful, loving, exciting, joyous, and meaningful...but it's not just up to God. If you don't believe it, it can't happen. Life can only play out as you deem fit.

Author Biography

Danielle Pashko has been working in the Nutrition, Wellness and Beauty industries for the past 15 years in New York City. As a licensed massage therapist, certified yoga instructor, nutritional consultant and thyroid cancer survivor, she fuses her modalities and personal experience to coach clients on how to live healthier, more fulfilling lives.

Danielle is the CEO of Pashko Wellness and provides consultations in Manhattan. She has taught and worked with clients in some of the world's leading spas and fitness clubs including The Sports Club LA, The Reebok Sports Club, Equinox Fitness, Exhale Spa and The Peninsula Spa. Her expertise in the wellness field has led to articles and videos on health and beauty for several publications including The NY Post, Yahoo Shine, The Jewish Week, Galtime, JCoach, Betty Confidential and NY Wellness Guide.

Made in the USA
Charleston, SC
29 May 2014